ANIMAL HOUSE STYLE

ANIMAL HOUSE STYLE

DESIGNING A HOME TO SHARE WITH YOUR PETS

JULIA SZABO

BULFINCH PRESS

NEW YORK · BOSTON

For all homeless pets who don't have an animal house of their own:
"Let each adopt one until there are none."

And for Samson and Tina Mae, d. 1996, Center for Animal Care & Control,
New York City: "I stop somewhere, waiting for you."

Bulfinch Press

Time Warner Book Group
1271 Avenue of the Americas, New York, NY 10020
Visit our Web site at www.bulfinchpress.com

First Edition
First Paperback Printing, 2005

Part of the joy of living with a pet is the unique character and personality of each animal. Because animals vary widely in terms of physical characteristics and care needs (even within the same species), it is important to consult with your pet's veterinarian before implementing any dietary or lifestyle changes discussed in this book. The information contained in this book is based upon sources that the author believes to be reliable. Information relating to individual products and companies is current as of February 1, 2001.

LIBRARY OF CONGRESS CATALOGING-IN-PUBLICATION DATA
Szabo, Julia.
    Animal house style: designing a home to share with your pets / Julia Szabo. — 1st ed.
        p. cm.
    ISBN 0-8212-5711-0
    1. Pets—Housing. 2. Dogs—Housing. 3. Cats—Housing. 4. Interior decoration. I. Title.
    SF414.2 .S92 2001
    636.08'31—dc21   2001025349

Designed by Bruce Campbell

PRINTED IN THE UNITED KINGDOM

CONTENTS

FOREWORD

*F*inally, proof that living with pets doesn't have to mean living with mess! *Animal House Style* offers easy, graceful decorating solutions that will inspire house-proud animal lovers to welcome pets into their homes. If you love animals, you'll love this book.

Mary Tyler Moore

INTRODUCTION

*P*erhaps it is inherent in being named Martha, but there has always lurked just below the surface of my being a frustrated interior decorator. Couple that with more than twenty years in the animal-shelter field, and it's easy to understand why I delight in the wonderful images that fill this book.

For those of us who work on behalf of animals less fortunate than those featured in *Animal House Style,* there is a poignancy as well. Here, you see how the most pampered of pooches can curl up on a costly kilim-upholstered chair without sending her human mom into instant cardiac arrest. In the world of animal shelters, we see dogs given up by their families for shedding on the new sofa. In *Animal House Style,* cats play atop museum-quality chairs, indulged by their caregivers. Outside the pages of this book, cats are too often declawed just so they won't mar the furniture.

Let's face it: Living with animals can present some interesting challenges. But whether it's behavioral problems, allergies, relocating a household, or removing muddy paw prints from the kitchen floor, it's nothing that can't be overcome with caring, creativity, and commitment. The Humane Society of the United States works to help pet owners maintain a loving bond with their animal companions. We offer advice and information on all aspects of pet care: finding pet-friendly rental housing, coping with pets and allergies, correcting unwanted behaviors. Our goal is to address pet problems before those problems separate pets from their families.

One of the things I love about this book is that it provides innovative, practical, and appealing solutions to so many problems related to having a pet and a beautiful living space, from fabric choices to cleaning products. *Animal House Style* sends a message to everyone who lives with an animal companion that it is possible to provide a comfortable home for pets while maintaining an attractive environment for the human members of the family. In fact, the most beautiful interiors are those shared with animals.

But *Animal House Style* is really about another kind of interior: the interior of the heart. The people and animals in this book share more than living space. Their relationships provide comfort that goes beyond the touch of lush fabrics and the beauty of fine furnishings. Theirs are deep, loving bonds that last for life.

That's the real message of *Animal House Style*. And it perfectly reflects and reinforces the message of the HSUS and of animal shelters around the country: Pets are for life, in every sense of the term. They share our lives. They enrich our lives. And we owe them nothing less than a lifelong commitment in return.

Martha C. Armstrong
Vice President for Companion Animals and Equine Protection
The Humane Society of the United States
Washington, D.C.

ANIMAL HOUSE STYLE

1.
WELCOME

*W*hether you call them pets or the more politically correct "companion animals," now is an exciting time to be sharing your home with furred, feathered, or finned creatures.

The Delta Society, an organization dedicated to improving human health through therapy and service animals, has sponsored studies proving conclusively that contact with animals affects human wellness in substantially positive ways, including lowering

blood pressure. Call it the laying-on of paws: Currently, scores of Americans have first-hand experience with the healing power of pets. It's estimated that some 64 million Americans are cat owners and about 62 million are dog owners. This doesn't include the millions of dogs and cats that go unaccounted for; the legions of people who share their homes with birds, ferrets, fish, rabbits, and other domesticated species; or the people who live with several different species of animal in one home. Whether you do the math or lose count, this country starts to look like a veritable animal kingdom!

That's a fact that helped many disgruntled voters get through the nail-biting year-2000 presidential race, as animal lovers took comfort in the knowledge that both candidates seemed to genuinely care about their family pets. If the Pledge of Allegiance's concept of "indivisible" took a beating with all that recounting, at least most Americans figured that regardless of the election's outcome, we'd still be one nation under dog.

As our appreciation of pets grows and we recognize just how valuable their friendship is to us, we are repaying the favor by making special accommodations for them as never

Opposite: Eleanor Mondale with one half of her animal family (from left): Celeste, Fiona, Lola, Millie, and Max.

before. Some of the world's most stylish people are creating pet-friendly interiors as attractive as they are comfortable. Whether traditional or modern, minimal or hyper-decorative, these interiors have one thing in common: Each room is approached as a communal nest for humans and animals — the four-legged residents' needs are not a decorating afterthought. Fashion designer and filmmaker Todd Oldham speaks for a fast-growing contingent of pet lovers when he says, "I designed my apartment to be my dog's home too. I made sure to design everything to be comfortable for her in every way, so we'd both be happy with the result." After they have taken a peek into Todd's home, and the homes of many like-minded animal lovers, I hope people will be inspired to be kinder to the animals they already know and the ones they may meet in the future. It's a fact that an elegant decor inspires us to take better care of our homes. I also believe that incorporating our pets' needs with our furnishings helps us to be kinder to all creatures: mongrels as well as purebreds, animals domesticated, wild, and ranched. And the kindness we put into practice can only be good for us, our communities, and our environment.

We Americans love feathering our nests, and we're now in the midst of a home-improvement boom. Television programs like *Antiques Roadshow* educate us about vintage treasures, while The Learning Channel's *Trading Spaces* lets us in on the well-guarded trade secrets of the country's top interior designers. At the same time, mass-market companies such as Banana Republic, Crate & Barrel, Ikea, Pottery Barn, and Target offer great design at affordable prices, inspiring and enabling us to create beautiful, functional interiors on even the tightest of budgets. And wouldn't you know, some of today's most compelling home-furnishings advertisements feature animals, from Baker's poetry-in-motion cavalier King Charles spaniel to Home Depot's rescued family of ducks to Marvin's sleepy bassett hound to George the cat, mascot of the now-defunct Furniture.com. Restoration Hardware always features dogs in its catalogs; Kroin Inc. of Cambridge, Massachusetts, makers of faucets, fixtures, and washbasins, recently ran a charming print ad that gave star billing to a yellow caique parrot. The Mitchell Gold Furniture Company's spokesdog is named Lulu; she's Mitchell's own English bulldog. Frankly, if you did a before-and-after story revealing a stylish interior with pets and the same interior without, you'd probably think that the petless version was missing something.

That's what Christina Grajales, an expert on midcentury modern furniture, discovered after adopting a mutt named Billie from the Humane Society of New York. It's hard to compete with the pristine beauty of Christina's choice (and very sought-after) Jean Prouvé furnishings, but the effervescent Billie manages to give the decor a unique per-

Opposite: At the home of architect Robin Elmslie Osler, a mutt named Uta lends character to a chair with a pedigree: the angular — and highly collectible — Florence Knoll armchair.

sonality that money and provenance cannot buy. Or consider Anya Larkin's splendid living room. With furniture by Donghia, Todd Hase, and Christian Liaigre; a plush Tibetan wool rug by Veedon Fleece; and gold-and-pewter-flecked wallpaper of Anya's design, it's as stylish as it can be. Or is it? Add Anya's beloved smooth-coated chow chow, Chloe, to the picture and you've got a much richer, more densely layered visual feast. Forget chinchilla bedspreads: Chloe's blue pelt makes her look like the most sumptuous luxury good in the world. She's a living, breathing "fun fur."

Sometimes our pets look so chic that it's hard to imagine a room — even a beautiful room — looking half as lovely without the special something ani-

mals bring to it. As I write this, my research associate, Cyrus the orange-eyed Persian cat, is curled up in front of the window with his head resting on a ceramic bonsai tree pot, pretty as a picture. Animals can be remarkably decorative. They bend themselves into beautiful shapes. They lend color, texture, and movement to a room, and generally enhance our environments. A chair without a cat on it is simply not as elegant as a chair with a cat on it — even if the chair in question was designed by LeCorbusier.

Unfortunately, an aesthetic appreciation of pets can be almost impossible to explain to the Realtor who holds the keys to the place you'd like to rent. If we remember one thing about the movie *Animal House,* it's the image of John Belushi yelling, "Food fight!" and the orgiastic chaos that ensues. Many people think of a home with pets as that kind of animal house, conjuring images of spectacular mess. Ask the average

Right: Magic happens — and interiors appear more beautiful — when the pets stay in the picture.

Above: Many pet owners deliberately style their furnishings to play up their pets' best features. Here, Chami and Beaji, author Barbara Taylor Bradford's bichons, really pop against the Biedermeier sofa's wine-dark upholstery.

Left: A wood table's high polish reflects the beauty of an Abyssinian named José.

Opposite: Gabriele Sanders and Timmy Haskell with three members of their multispecies family: Blaze the dalmatian, Layla the kitten, and Leeloo the Moluccan cockatoo.

landlord why he or she won't rent to people with pets, and the answer is always the same: They trash the place.

On the topic of movies, perhaps you've seen or heard about the Maysles brothers' 1975 film *Grey Gardens*. This classic documentary depicts a mother and daughter, both named Edie (the aunt and first cousin, respectively, of Jacqueline Kennedy Onassis), who lived with countless cats, plus a few well-fed raccoons, in a Hamptons house so neglected the town moved to evict them from their own home. Unfortunately, a *Grey Gardens* stigma attaches itself like a stubborn barnacle to those who share their home with more than one or two pets. If they're not "crazy cat ladies," they're another C-word: collectors, defined as people who take in more animals than they are able to care for, and both people and pets wind up living in appalling squalor.

But all over the country, people are debunking the myth that pet owners — especially those who live with more than two animals — are filthy, slovenly, wacky, or downright beastly. The ones I've had the pleasure of getting to know are more responsible, more socially aware, more aesthetically fine-tuned than their petless counterparts. They're also more glamorous than any human has a right to be! Recent studies reveal that people who have pets live measurably longer than those who don't have pets. Meanwhile, anecdotal evidence I've compiled suggests that pet people also lead more stylish lives. How do they do it? On the following pages, you'll see: through a combination of common sense, basic animal-handling skills, patience, and love.

Gabriele Sanders is a textbook example of an upstanding tenant. She pays her rent on time . . . she keeps her unit spotless . . . she's respectful of her neighbors, never making loud noises late in the evening. Every December, she fashions a festive holiday wreath of fragrant eucalyptus to hang in the hallway for the benefit of the building's other residents. Ironically, most landlords wouldn't rent to Gabriele because she has pets. A lot of pets, in fact: two dogs, three cats, and three birds (an umbrella cockatoo, an Australian rose-breasted cockatoo, and a pigeon she rescued and rehabilitated; when given a window of opportunity to return to the wild, the pigeon came back). In his book *Architecture Without Architects,* the esteemed Bernard Rudofsky ponders whether Noah's ark was a boat or a building. Whichever, it was the ur–animal house — and Gabriele is a latter-day Noah. Okay, so her ark doesn't float; it's securely moored to a trendy loft building. Yet far from being a cramped poop deck, her multispecies surroundings are airy, sleek, and — believe it or not — *white!* It's such an attractive interior that *Elle Decor* has featured it no fewer than three times, once on the cover. Animal houses and their residents are turning up in the glossiest magazines with increasing fre-

Left: Photographer Carlton Davis makes sure to spend quality time with his very sociable king snake, Jazz. If you can't provide TLC for a reptile, don't acquire one.

quency: here, a dog on an ultramodern sofa; there, a cat on a traditional Louis XVI armchair, watching a nature video about fish.

In my travels, I've been lucky to meet and profile countless people of great style — people like Gabriele — who would do anything for their pets. According to the most basic requirements of any animal-shelter adoption agreement, for cats we're supposed to provide food, water, and shelter; and for dogs, food, water, and shelter, plus the opportunity for daily fresh air and exercise. Birds require a clean, spacious cage; fish need a clean, spacious aquarium. Reptiles, such as iguanas, require much more than most people can give them: a warm, humid climate approximating that of the tropics they came from, a healthy diet of fresh veggies, and plenty of space in which to stretch out. Tragically, pet shops sell iguanas cheap, touting them as "the perfect starter pet," and many wind up literally tossed out with the trash. Animal lovers ought to do their

Above left: With a puppy's playful irreverence, Prudence Designs arranged dogwood and curly willow in Alvar Aalto's iconic vase, tying Blue Seal dog biscuits to the branches with raffia cord.

Above right: Chris Madden's Winnie feels right at home on Bassett's West Highland chair, created with her in mind.

Above: A couple of silver foxes: the legendary French furniture designer Pierre Paulin and one of his two Akitas, Otomi, relax on Paulin's glamorous Ribbon chair.

best to discourage the impulse acquisition of reptiles — which is why, beautiful though they are, you won't find any iguanas in this book.

But more and more, animal lovers are going way beyond the basics by indulging our pets. We feed them expensive gourmet foods and buy them posh designer toys, beds, bowls, collars, sweaters, and raincoats. We provide day-care opportunities so our pets can socialize and play while we're busy at the office. We carry our pets' photos in our wallets; make appointments with veterinary specialists, pet psychics, acupuncturists, and massage therapists; and hire the services of pet trainers, pet photographers, pet nutritionists, and pet shrinks. In New York City, where absolutely nothing raises eyebrows, there's even a pet florist. Prudence Designs, named for the owners' dachshund, is happy to spruce up arrangements sent to dog lovers with . . . dog biscuits!

So why is there no such thing as a pet decorator? Because pets themselves are natural-born interior designers. Their work is based on instinct, and those of us who live with pets can learn a lot from animals about design for living — if only we'd heed the lessons they have to teach us. I know that my dogs and cats taught me how to design a comfortable, high-performance interior. And across the country, others are learning from their pets as well.

Interior designers are some of the savviest creative types around. No wonder so many of them live with pets: They appreciate the free style counsel their four-legged friends offer up daily! Even animals in the wild display architectural tendencies. Cliff swallows, for instance, build clay houses that look like little jugs, I'm told by Stan Wan, who photographed some of the beautiful images you'll see on these pages. Maybe domesticated animals aren't master builders in a league with the cliff swallows, but they certainly are decorators. Consult a design pro and chances are he or she lives with a pet — like Mayer Rus, editor of *Interior Design* magazine, who goes everywhere with his scene-stealing bull terrier, Louise, or *Nest* magazine's Joseph Holtzman and his poodle, Guido. Phillip Miller, of America Dural Interior Design in Cambridge, Massachusetts, lives *and* works with a pet: Otis the Manchester terrier is the office mascot, adding his *je ne sais quoi* to the window display and greeting guests as they come through the door. The successful interior-design firm Brown, Siegel was formed after its principals, Nanette Brown and Stephen Miller Siegel, met walking their dogs in New York's Central Park. Marco and Rachael Olmi's interior-design concern, Catoe & Bambu, was named after a

Siamese cat (Catoe) and a dog (Bambu, now deceased). Catoe and Titta, a mutt, make themselves right at home at the Olmis' elegant store-showroom in New York City, amid a selection of midcentury modern furnishings that includes chairs by Fritz Hansen and Paul McCobb. Author and home-decorating guru Chris Madden has created stylish, dog-friendly interiors for the likes of Oprah Winfrey and makes regular appearances on the *Today Show* with another famous client, Katie Couric. In her furniture collection for Bassett, Chris designed something special inspired by her dog, Winnie. Upholstered in red-and-tan plaid, the West Highland chair looks its best with a West Highland terrier proudly seated on it. (If you'll pardon the pun, Winnie is a real Bassett hound!) Tails in Need is a nonprofit animal-welfare organization based in New York City; its cofounders are the aptly named decorators Kitty Hawks and Bunny Williams!

In my spare time, I do a fair amount of animal rescue. That's how I became intimate with a reality that's far removed from the glossy, perfectly styled biosphere of shelter magazines. I'm talking about the gritty world of animal shelters, where dogs and cats are held in no-frills concrete kennels until, if they're lucky, someone comes to take them home. Considering where many of these animals came from, shelters are often the most humane environment — and the only interior — they've ever known. *Country Living* is one of my favorite magazines because not only does it feature pets in almost every story, it even runs a column called "You and Your Pet." But driving through rural areas, I've seen a very different side of country living: starving cats wandering into the road and dogs chained outdoors without so much as an uninsulated dog house for warmth. Shelters across this country are overburdened because there are more people abandoning animals than adopting them. And so, in a scandalous waste of life, millions of intelligent, sensitive, beautiful creatures are euthanized every year — animals that could easily have brought smiles and confidence to children, comfort and cheer to the elderly, or assistance to the physically challenged.

When an animal is brought to a shelter, paperwork is filled out that asks for an explanation. One of the most common reasons given at shelters for abandoning a pet is "He wrecked the furniture." That's bad enough, but there's more. Of all the other lame excuses offered — "Can't care for," "We had a baby," "We're moving" — the most appalling has to be this: "We redecorated, and now *it* doesn't match the furniture." (I couldn't believe this either at first, but there's plenty of evidence to confirm that it's true.) This saddens me like nothing else. For as decorative as pets can be, they are not "its," pretty accessories to be disposed of on an aesthetic whim. Fashion is fleeting; the love a pet offers should be cherished forever. If you're thinking of acquiring an animal

Below: Architect Denis Colomb created the Neptune rug to match the blue gray coat of Neptune, his Burmese cat. A fringe benefit: When Neptune sheds on it, the hairs are barely noticeable.

just because of the exotic way the animal looks, you're barking up the wrong tree. (Incidentally, the adorable dog who plays Eddie on TV's *Frasier* — in real life he's called Moose — was a tornado of destruction who chewed his way through two homes before settling down with his beloved Mathilde DeCagney, the woman who adopted him and trains him for the show.)

Sadly, despite all we know about the extraordinary things pets do for our physical and emotional well-being, there are many people who still value inanimate objects more than living, breathing, loyal best friends. It's my hope that the interiors featured in this book will prove that pets and fine furnishings can coexist happily — and that it's infinitely more chic to keep our friends close than to give up on them. With a little ingenuity and lots of patience, we can tailor our homes to meet our pets' needs, creating interiors as beautiful as they are functional — interiors only enhanced by the playful activity of critters large and small. All the people profiled in these pages share one thing in common: It's their firm belief that a house simply isn't a home until it's an animal house. "The secret to living in style with animals," explains eyewear designer Robert Marc, "is to love your pet more than your possessions." Would that all people thought that way!

As a baby, she learned how to walk "because our collie got up to get away from me — probably because I was pestering her! — and I followed." When she lived with her parents in the vice president's residence in Washington, D.C., her family had another collie, a beagle mix, and two cats. Today, Eleanor Mondale shares a farm in the Hamptons called Green Acres with her doctor boyfriend, Joe DeBellis, plus two rottweilers (Fiona and Max), a mastiff mix (Celeste) adopted from a nearby shelter called A.R.F., two cats (Steve and Joey) adopted from the East Quogue Animal Shelter, an umbrella cockatoo (Pebbles), two miniature horses (Millie and Lola), and two full-size rescued Thoroughbreds (Sam and Charlie).

Eleanor is a super-Noah who embodies the live-and-let-live aesthetic crucial to a happy animal house. Don't even think of trying this at home: She has over thirty years' experience training and handling animals; she even managed to train her bird to give a warning when she's about to poop! Eleanor will bring her mini horses indoors for the occasional living-room visit without wiping their hooves. Despite all this, her place looks smashing.

I'm not going to say that decorating with pets is easy; it takes creativity and lots of work. But the new breed of pet lover enjoys rising to the challenge. It's often said that necessity is the mother of invention. Well, necessity must have grown up in an animal house: So many great new inventions for stylish, practical living come out of homes with pets that I suspect you'll get something useful out of this book whether you have animals or not. Eleanor Mondale and people like her — and there are more of them out there than you may suspect! — are proving all the naysayers wrong by creating interiors so well groomed they make many petless places look shaggy by comparison. In short, they're giving the term "animal house" a whole new spin.

Seeing the stylish way people are living with animals, maybe more landlords will take a chance on pet people without being disappointed. Of course, it's up to us animal-loving tenants to make sure our homes look and smell great. Call me Pollyanna, but I'm confident the day isn't far off when the tide will *really* turn and some smart real estate developer will act on the knowledge that pet people would prefer fellow pet people for neighbors (instead of litigious tenants who make complaints about imaginary pet noise, odor, and filth). Already, the San Francisco SPCA receives thousands of inquiries each month from landlords, tenants, and animal groups interested in its Open Door program, designed to help people find "Pets OK" rental housing and raise awareness of the many benefits provided by pets in rental housing. Meanwhile, in New York City, a Realtor called the Corcoran Group has employed noted animal trainer and author Bash Dibra to help clients' dogs pass the dreaded co-op board interview, with a high rate of success. I'm optimistic that soon we'll see ground broken for a full-service luxury high-rise built exclusively for animal lovers. There'd be several banks of spacious elevators, soundproofed walls, terraces with pet-safe guardrails, an on-premises vet ready to make emergency house calls, a twenty-four-hour pet-supply store, a day-care center complete with canine gym and swimming pool, and a concierge with the phone numbers of reputable dog walkers and cat- and bird-sitters at his fingertips. Of course, the awning out front would read — what else? — "Animal House."

Until that house is built, we have this one. Enjoy your stay!

2.
CRITTER COMFORTS

"Consider yourself at home," goes the song from the musical *Oliver.* "Consider yourself part of the furniture." Animals have made themselves right at home in our collective heart, getting under our skin and weaving themselves into the fabric of our lives. Literally: It's virtually impossible to have an animal house without Helmac Products Corporation's Evercare Pet Hair Pic-Up, a roll of sticky tape with a handle that enables pet lovers to remove evidence of shedding (which can make the unrolled look as if they live in fur-lined kennels). In Carl Reiner's *2000 Year Old Man,* the title character is asked to name the greatest invention of all time. He says it's Saran Wrap, but the Pet Hair Pic-Up gets my vote.

It's safe to say that animals *are* part of the furniture. Sometimes they even start to look and behave like home furnishings. A freshly groomed cocker spaniel, for instance, takes on the appearance of a cushy ottoman; tiny lapdog breeds are called "teacups." My patient dog Sam permits his rump to double as a headrest while I'm sofa-bound, reading or watching TV. On freezing-cold nights, when they do me the honor of sleeping with me, my heat-seeking and -generating cats form the most thermally efficient comforter imaginable. After a long walk, I'm always amused at the sight of my dog Pepper stretched out on her stomach, flatter than Wile E. Coyote, on the hardwood floor. She looks more like a rug than a dog. And when she hears her name, her body stays still as her tail wags furiously back and forth: She's an area rug with a built-in metronome.

Odd as it may seem, viewing our pets as furniture is a valuable exercise, because successfully furnishing an animal house requires adopting a new perspective on furniture.

We think we know the basic criteria of a good chair or a serviceable sofa. But if we have pets, the list of criteria lengthens. Any designs we bring home must be extra functional, performing beautifully while still looking great. "Critter comforts" — the cozy feeling we share with our beloved beasts — is a phrase that perfectly captures the guiding philosophy of animal-house furnishings. That philosophy is all about sharing the comforts of home with our pets.

Pet lovers approach individual items of furniture quite differently from the way our petless counterparts do. Most people, for instance, look at Ligne Roset's très chic Dolce Vita chaise and see a sculptural, cutting-edge trophy piece. But restaurateur Marco Maccioni, of Le Cirque 2000 and Osteria del Circo fame, saw a well-made lounge sturdy enough to support himself *and* Mostro, his 130-pound bull mastiff (whose awesome size makes him look like an imposing piece of furniture, with paws as huge as the claw feet on a retro bathtub).

At the (much) lower end of the price scale is another example of performance furniture, a popular chair that happens to be named for a critter: the butterfly. A relic of the 1950s, the striking butterfly chair has been updated by Crate & Barrel with an easy-to-fold steel frame and washable, interchangeable cotton covers in a range of colors and patterns. It meets the three criteria every style-conscious pet owner looks for in a piece

Right: We're not suggesting that you use fine furnishings as a venue for games of tug — but don't tell that to Marco Maccioni and Mostro.

Above: Knuks the ferret really digs her Crate & Barrel butterfly chair.

of animal-house furniture: It looks terrific, it's widely available, and it won't break the bank. It's also very ferret friendly. Ferret lovers know that their sweet little pets love nothing more than to hang out in hammocks à la *Gilligan's Island*. Sure, there are tiny ferret-specific hammocks available at pet stores (they retail for anywhere from $15 to $40, depending on material). But a design snob would sniff at the very idea of decorating a room with them. The butterfly chair, on the other hand, is essentially a good-looking ferret hammock big enough for a person; when the ferret gets bored with the chair, his human can occupy it too. The lesson: For a home with ferrets, a butterfly chair is as cost effective as it is chic. (Other ferret-friendly options include the butterfly's cousin, the Lampa Circular Chair, available in two sizes, and Blu Dot's handsome, hammocklike Felt-Up chair, which is essentially a sling made of gray felt.)

So what does the average ferret think of the butterfly hammock, er, chair? See for yourself. To the left is a white jill called Knuks ("skunk" spelled backward), one of several ferrets belonging to *Modern Ferret Magazine* editor Mary Shefferman. I practically grew up looking at an Ingres painting in the Metropolitan Museum of Art called *Princesse de Broglie,* and something about the sight of Knuks lounging happily in her bright blue chair like pampered, porcelain-complexioned royalty reminds me of the princess.

We can appreciate good design, but can our pets? The answer is an unequivocal *yes.* Our beasts have much in common with Huckleberry Finn: We can adopt them, but we can't entirely civilize them. Even perfectly trained pets are and always will be wild at heart. They bark, pant, drool, growl, and eat things that frequently dismay us (horse manure and insects, to name just two). Still, experience tells us that animals are remarkably adept at making themselves at home on our turf. Their five senses govern their actions outside, but in the great indoors they display a remarkable sixth sense for luxury. When it comes to fine furnishings, many pets are civilized to the point of being connoisseurs. They often display astonishing refinement, sitting cross-legged with Emily Post delicacy (an endearing gesture interior designer Michael Levinson calls "lady paws"). All species have a remarkable talent for trading up that's part of their survival instinct. My cat Huey was rescued from a collector who'd kept some forty cats in a small, filthy room until all of them developed virulent upper-respiratory infections.

When Huey finally came home with me after a long stay at the vet, healthy and strong, he promptly commandeered a chair upholstered in extremely pricy Scalamandré leopard-patterned fabric. It's been his observation tower ever since.

Let's face it: Our animals have evolved to become so domesticated that a furnished interior is their natural habitat. Fortunately for them, the climate is much better controlled indoors than it is outside. That comes in especially handy for certain animals, such as the Chihuahua, Chinese Crested dog, or hairless Sphinx cat, who get cold easily. And while some animals are content to lie on the bare floor before a roaring fire, others have us wrapped around their little paws until we spare no expense in indulging their expensive tastes. Case in point: me and my brindle pit bull, Britannia Tige (B for short).

When I first met her, B was an anxious resident of an animal shelter, rescued by animal control from a lifetime of being chained in a filthy basement. After gazing once into those amber eyes fringed with Shetland-pony lashes, I knew she'd be coming home with me — but the shelter wisely decreed that B couldn't go home until she'd been spayed. So I left her for the longest day of my life with a Mexican horse blanket I keep in the car, to take the chill off the kennel's concrete floor. That was only the beginning of B's reeducation in the fine art of living well.

Shortly after B came home, I got the assignment to profile designer John Yunis's place for *Elle Decor*. I'd told him about my new B-loved, and to my surprise he invited me to bring her along for our interview. Upon arrival, my dog made a B-line for John's splendid bed, covered and canopied in plush silvery gray velvet. She began rolling luxuriantly on her back, becoming one with the sumptuous fabric as if velvet were her natural element. Then she rested her head on his pillow!

Ever since, B has demanded the best. While researching an article for the *New York Post*, I borrowed a glamorous Lucite dog bed that Gucci designer Tom Ford created for John, his Jack Russell terrier. Even before the hunk of designer Lucite arrived, I had an inkling as to which member of my furry family would claim it as her own. Despite the black cotton cushion cover's being a magnet for her coppery hairs, B loved it — so much so that I keenly felt her resentment for months after I had to give it back. (Eventually, I broke down and bought one for her.) B's love of luxury might have something to do with her bullishness; anyone born under the sign of the bull (i.e., Taurus) tends to take great comfort in beautiful things. According to Cydney Cross of the not-for-profit pit bull rescue group Out of the Pits, "Pit bulls are creature-comfort dogs. They love sitting on chairs and cushions with blankets wrapped around them. They definitely don't like being cold and wet! It makes me laugh when people say these dogs

34

feel no pain, because of all the animals I've worked with, they're the ones that most want to get cozy."

Considering her appreciation of the finer things, B deserves to be the official mascot of Luxuryfinder.com. But, believe it or not, she isn't the most pampered dog in New York. That distinction goes to Sweetie, a little mutt whose humans, John Bartlett and Mark Welsh, found her one night on a deserted country road, took her in, and changed their lives forever. Sweetie has her own column in *Elle* magazine (Mark serves as her interpreter), where she holds forth on such subjects as "the paradox of being naked and wearing fur." She's close girlfriends with the actress Sarah Jessica Parker and spent the afternoon before the 2000 Oscars hanging with Hilary Swank, Minnie Driver, and Sandra Bullock as they prepped for the big night. She recently authored her life story, but Sweetie hasn't forgotten her roots; she does her share of philanthropic work by serving as the "First Lady" of a Long Island shelter called the North Shore Animal League. Still, like any socialite, she can't very well be expected to loaf around on some old crochet afghan — so hers is a pillow covered in fabulous Missoni fabric.

When Joe Dolce and Jonathan Burnham brought home two puppies from the Animal Rescue Fund (A.R.F.) shelter in East Hampton, they didn't drive themselves crazy looking for dog cushions handsome enough to fit in with their George Nelson table, Donghia sofa, and lanterns by Noguchi and Marcel Wanders. The guys simply gave the pups the sleek black meditation cushions they use for yoga and called it a day.

The smart companies are the ones that promote a seamless blend of human and pet lifestyles, recognizing that the four-legged and two-legged share an equal stake in a cozy,

Left: Suddenly, "It's a dog's life" takes on a whole new meaning: Sweetie on her Missoni floor cushion.

well-appointed home. A perfect example of critter comforts in action on the selling floor may be found at any Restoration Hardware store. The company deserves praise for its uniquely dog-friendly approach to selling home furnishings. For instance, in addition to offering tennis balls big enough that large dogs won't be in danger of choking on them, Restoration sells a rubber boot mat that, the company boasts, doubles as a pet-food place mat! Restoration Hardware and clever companies like it are producing home furnishings that pets and their humans can share in style. Being salt-of-the-earth types, most pet lovers don't mind sitting on the floor. I'm convinced that floor cushions are trendy these days — whether they're covered in canvas or leather — because so many of us don't think twice about joining our dogs on the floor. As I write this, one of

Pottery Barn's most popular products is a square floor cushion that looks for all the world like a deluxe dog bed (and a particularly handsome one at that). At around $50, it's cheaper than certain overpriced doggy pillows sold at pet-supply shops. I've tried in vain to purchase one or more, but the item is consistently sold out — probably to other dog lovers.

While most cat-bed manufacturers produce cheap-looking circular foam objects, leave it to Martha Stewart to create a lovely cat bed, a rectangular tufted cushion covered in a washable ivory herringbone that blends with many types of decor. Martha's cat bed looks so much like an expensive, high-style cushion that it wouldn't be out of place next to a designer sofa in the home of someone who doesn't have cats!

Angela Adams, meanwhile, designs floor cushions of appliqué Ultrasuede and patchwork faux fur, in vibrant color combinations such as brown, orange, and pink. Adams's fashionable, machine-washable pillows are created for people, but she's obviously got felines on her mind: The styles are named for her own and her friends' cats, who love to nap on them.

When I was growing up in the seventies, one piece of furniture occupied pride of place in my room: a beanbag chair with an apple green vinyl cover. I loved that thing, but I was always irritated at the way my legs stuck to the vinyl (and now, of course, I'm shocked that I ever liked anything in such a tacky shade of green). Obviously, Ed Rigaud had the same experience. His company, Eazy Bean, has successfully updated that classic of seventies decor with removable brushed-cotton twill and Ultrasuede covers in lovely colors for an elegant take on the beanbag. Besides being plush, comfortable seating for kids of all ages, Eazy Beans double as dog beds to drool over. The one that lives in the center of my living room — actually, we call it the wag room — has proven so popular with visitors of the human and canine persuasion that it's obvious I'll have to invest in a few more.

Why shouldn't we incorporate special places for pets into our surroundings, places that are theirs and theirs alone? This means sizing up our spaces and finding spots for our friends to make their own. Laurie Smith, an interior designer based in Jackson,

Above: Your dog bed or mine? It wasn't designed as a dog bed, but the Mitchell Gold Company's Malory floor pillow works equally well for man and beast. Just ask the company spokesbulldog, Lulu.

Above: Eazy Bean's Low Lounger in taupe (foreground) earns the pit bull seal of approval.

Mississippi, who's a star of TV's *Trading Spaces,* has done just that for Chelsea, her black Lab. "I believe every pet needs a den, a cozy little space *inside* the house that they feel is theirs," Laurie explains. "It's important to make pets feel like they're truly part of the family, and to give them a place they can retreat to that's their own space, just like the other family members. In our house, we converted a closet under a staircase by carpeting it in seagrass, which vacuums clean easily. In the winter, Chelsea's bed has a fleece cover; in summer, we change it to a cotton cover with a leather top, which helps keep her cool. She loves to retreat there, especially when she hears thunder outside!"

Being arboreal, cats naturally seek high places, and their extraordinary agility means they can pretty much climb wherever they like, whether it's a high shelf or the top of a chest of drawers. My Cyrus, for instance, loves hanging out on top of the television set, which sits on an antique table. I have a series of snapshots taken of him while *The Poseidon Adventure* was on; incredibly, the little guy dozed through the entire movie, completely oblivious to all that disaster, destruction, and overacting.

The highest most dogs get is the sofa, and many canines, once up there, take on the air of intrepid explorers, staking their claim to these cushioned seas of tranquility like so many four-legged Neil Armstrongs. So why do we let them, when training them not to isn't difficult? Because nothing is more amusing than seeing fido flopped out on the sofa. Our couch hounds give us a daily lesson in the fine art of relaxation — and a reminder that we must always make room in our busy schedules for down time. Some breeds absolutely require a sofa to be happy. "I've got five greyhounds who certainly enjoy their new life as couch potatoes," says Robin Norton, founder of Greysland, an organization that rescues these wonderful dogs after they've been retired from the racetrack.

The sofa is without question most people's biggest furniture investment, and a key element of any interior. In an animal house, however, the couch is also the embodiment of critter comforts, an upholstered landmark that magnetically draws pets to nest on, in, and behind it.

Keep in mind when selecting your sofa that small dogs don't make much of a dent, but large dogs displace the upholstery significantly. A round, tight upholstery style is preferable to an incredible sinking sofa. Fiberfill-stuffed cushions are a much better bet than down because synthetic fillings "recover" after impact much faster than feathers. And wood accents should be kept to a minimum. All that explains why I selected a vintage three-piece sectional sofa by Heywood-Wakefield, circa 1950.

Left: On Simon Doonan's sofa, a Norwich terrier called Liberace displays kinship with his namesake, surrounded by Jonathan Adler pillows in razzle-dazzle colors.

Below: Murray zones out on "his" end of Michael Levinson's sofa.

Right: Moxie's preferred hangout is "the roundhouse" — the secure nook behind Charlotte Frieze's sofa and loveseat, both covered in Clarence House fabric.

Each piece is quite sturdy, heavy enough to withstand being tackled by more than one big, muscular dog; the only wood accents are the legs, which are set too low to suffer dings and tooth marks; and besides, the Pee-wee Herman fan in me appreciated that the profile on each section looks like a big, smiling dog.

Where you place your sofa is as important as what sofa style you select. In the world of interiors, Peter Vaughn is known as the man who rediscovered the spare, colorful designs of the late Baron Alessandro Albrizzi, who was active in the 1960s and '70s. Surrounded by haute furnishings, Dewey, Peter's adorable West Highland white terrier, was bound to become a connoisseur. Not surprisingly, his selection of a favorite spot on the Rose Cumming chenille-covered sofa clearly displays his astute command of his surroundings. "From the northwest corner of the sofa, Dewey can see all the major entrances and exits," Peter explains. "It's a very secure point for him, because he has the wall in back of him, so he feels protected. And he's up high enough that he can look out the window and be aware of what's going on outdoors."

Now that we've become accustomed to a new way of seeing furniture — from the viewpoint of our pets' comfort as well as our own — it's time to expand our perspective to look at each room as a high-performance interior.

The good news: Now that we know how to go about selecting well-designed furnishings we can all share, we can start to relax. As millions of us learn firsthand about the joys of living with animals, notions of preserving certain spaces for special occasions are fast becoming obsolete. Once upon a time, people closed off the "good" living room as if it were an extremely

41

precious wing of a museum, banishing anyone or anything from the premises that might carry the risk of entropy (i.e., children and pets) and designating a casual den as the everyday family hangout. Thankfully, that's ancient history now. These days, we shun touch-me-not furnishings — i.e., expanses of silk — in favor of furniture that functions. "To design an environment for living without the idea that pets are going to be part of the landscape is not really designing for real life," says Joey Jagod, director of design at Eziba.com. Peter Vaughn agrees: "I grew up in a house where we could put our feet on anything," he says, "and furniture was meant to be used, not protected." Where author and *House Beautiful* editor Lisa Fine grew up, she recalls, "the thinking was, if it wasn't good for the dog, then why have it?"

More and more, that kind of live-and-let-live approach prevails. Why? Because if you spend time worrying about stains and spills, you're existing, not living. It's much more fun to have a living room you feel comfortable living in. "I refuse to alter my lifestyle in the name of preserving the decor," declares Michael Levinson. Fittingly, his Lab mix, Murray, is allowed absolutely everywhere in his home, which is decorated with nineteenth-century American Empire antiques acquired through years of scouring auction houses and estate sales. The home of architect Robin Elmslie Osler, by contrast, is notable for its mouth-watering collection of midcentury modernist furniture — the very originals many of us covet at vintage stores and auctions: Eames fiberglass chairs and wooden screens, leather chairs and sofas by Florence Knoll, a George Nelson stereo. Robin inherited many of these originals from her parents, and they're extremely valuable collectors' items. Yet not one is off-limits to Robin's two mutts, Dagmar and Uta, or Juve the calico cat. Sure, there's the occasional scratch here and there. But the patina of time and wear only proves how enduring these design icons really are.

Paul Mansour is one of the most house-proud people I've met — so much so that his walls are lined with framed photographs from his local historical society

of the way his 1907 home used to look. Interior designer Susan McCabe updated those traditional interiors, riffing off the colors — green, gold, and red — of the exterior and the extraordinary oak moldings, all original to this structure that combines many architectural styles: French eclectic Tudor, American Craftsman, and Adirondack bungalow. The Henredon manor-style sofa holds up extremely well under a cat's pouncing paws, as does the center-hung brass curtain rod that serves as a sturdy high-wire for a feline Wallenda. "I basically chose everything with longevity in mind," explains Susan, who shares her own home with Elsa, a rambunctious Old English sheepdog. The resulting habitat is as hospitable to a bachelor as it is to Ollo, Paul's tabby — yet still permits room for change. "If Paul wanted to," Susan adds, "he could move a nice, big, hairy black dog in there and everything would be fine."

A laissez-faire lifestyle permits a lot more than sharing one's home with animals. It enables you to have friends over whenever the spirit moves you, to host worry-free parties, and to entertain out-of-town visitors. And all that doesn't diminish quality of life; quite the opposite.

Happily, pet lovers are opting to live with treasured objects rather than consigning them to storage where they're safe from harm. The Danish designer Arne Jacobsen was responsible for creating many of the modernist icons that beautify our contemporary design landscape; the originals can be found in the design collection of New York's Museum of Modern Art (MoMA) and new ones continue to be produced by Knoll. Despite the availability of brand-new Jacobsen chairs, vintage originals — even examples with torn and stained upholstery — continue to command high prices at antiques stores and auctions.

Jacobsen's graceful Swan chair floats serenely in the home of Jean-Claude Huon, who enjoys swiveling it on its metal base for the amusement of his Abyssinian cat, Zulla. The chair is covered in a woven wool that's definitely not recommended for high-traffic pawing — but, like many stylish pet lovers, Jean-Claude is vehemently opposed to declawing.

On the subject of museums and chairs, I had the pleasure of seeing Wiener Werkstatte founder Josef Hoffmann's beautiful art nouveau café table and chairs at a 1986 MoMA exhibition, "Vienna 1900." Those designs left a big impression on me. Although Hoffmann's style has been copied a million times over, and versions of his designs pop up in cafés throughout Europe, I never thought I'd see the beautiful originals in a place where I could actually touch them — until I visited the home of fashion designer Han Feng. Her spacious Manhattan loft is home to a Hoffmann table, plus three Hoffmann chairs and a loveseat, all with their original upholstery intact. What's more, she actually uses them — and far from wigging out when her dog and two cats want to play in the vicinity, she dangles a silk ribbon to get them going.

If you're determined to furnish your animal house with antiques made of wood, go for lighter-colored finishes, avoiding deep, dark grains (such as the precious and costly wenge, or anything stained to look like it). Dark woods call more attention to scratches. Also, it's a good idea to keep on hand plenty of liquid scratch cover from the hardware store to help minimize the appearance of nicks and dings.

3.
GET DOWN

*D*r. Stanley Coren, professor of psychology at the University of British Columbia and author of *How to Speak Dog,* is one of the world's most respected dog authorities. So when he told me that creating a performance interior for pets is "all about flooring," I was all ears.

The floor is where our pets spend a lot of time, whether or not they're allowed on the furniture. It's also the place where most accidents occur. That's why the majority of ani-

mal houses have bare floors — especially homes with birds, where guano is par for the course. "You can't have a bird if you can't deal with guano," points out novelist Sheri Holman, who shares her home with a charismatic mustache parakeet named Ibrahim. Wood floors make guano cleanup a cinch, even if you have more than one bird.

"I kept my floors bare for him," says Marco Maccioni, indicating Mostro, his bull mastiff. That's because Mostro's 130 pounds would easily displace any rug he set foot on! Bare doesn't have to mean barren, however. They're the first choice for performance, but bare floors are not as plain-Jane as they sound. The parquet floors in the Summer Palace in Saint Petersburg are a great example: They're extraordinarily decorative, with several tones of wood artfully combined to create dazzling patterns fit for a tsar. Wood floors look great in a variety of finishes: bleached, stained dark, left au naturel. Wood can run the gamut of styles from ultramodern to traditional, coordinating smoothly with all types of furniture. And as long as it's covered with a polyurethane finish, wood is easy to keep clean with regular mopping and/or vacuuming. Then

Right: Designer Peter McGrattan and his German shepherd, Roxanne, enjoy a unique floor treatment: the yellowed pages of an old book, protected by several coats of polyurethane.

there's the wide variety of good-looking, widely available wood laminates, such as Pergo, not to mention durable prefinished wood flooring from Husky Hardwood Floors (they're easy to remember because their logo is a handsome husky dog).

Some pet lovers like to paint their wood floors. Gabriele Sanders's floorboards are white, and they've become charmingly distressed, farmhouse style, by the pitter-patter of big-toenailed feet (thanks to a Rhodesian Ridgeback named Monroe and a dalmatian named Blaze). Robin Elmslie Osler, on the other hand, has painted different sections of her floor with Ralph Lauren paint colors in dark blue, gray, and yellow, and covered the whole thing with a polyurethane finish to help keep it looking new.

Just because there's no rug on the floor doesn't mean there can't be pattern. If you're feeling creative, why not paint designs on the wood floor with polyurethane paint? For an even more offbeat option, take a page out of Peter McGrattan's book. The designer papered his unsightly wood floors with yellowed pages taken from two copies of an old edition of Gibbon's *The Decline and Fall of the Roman Empire,* then varnished the whole thing with several coats of polyurethane. "It starts on page one and goes right through, in sequence," Peter says of his literary-historical decoupage. The lovely end result is the equivalent of wallpaper for the floor — and it's more decorative than any carpet. Some might think the inventor of such an exquisite floor treatment would guard his creation against wear and tear, but Peter is happy to share the artwork underfoot with Roxanne, the German shepherd he adopted from the ASPCA.

Ceramic tiles are an optimal choice for any animal house. Not only are they blissfully easy to keep clean, they stay cool — a big plus for dogs who suffer in hot weather even when the air-conditioning is turned up to the max. Be sure to select a dark grout, as Anya Larkin did with her ceramic tiles from D&W Flooring, whose rich green hue is a deliberate homage to the nineteenth-century Arts and Crafts movement. Slate squares are ideal for dirt hiding (especially in an urban environment), ease of maintenance, elegance, and summer pet comfort.

Concrete makes an excellent flooring that also happens to be very cooling for pets in the summertime. Author and music producer Kohle Yohannan's home had a past life as a body shop. The pet-friendly highlight of his place is the concrete floor left over from its previous incarnation. After Kohle had the concrete cleaned and polished, the result was flooring so low-maintenance that when he fell in love with a mastiff mix, he didn't have to think twice about adopting him. (What's more, he didn't need to make any changes to his decor before bringing the dog home.) At Han Feng's loft, meanwhile, the low-maintenance concrete floors are so decorative they put one in mind of a wall-to-wall painting by the artist Ross Bleckner — and they're extremely forgiving of dirt.

Above: With her heavy, warm coat, it's no wonder Nadia the cream chow chow likes to park on the cool ceramic tile floor, surrounded by Donghia dining chairs.

Right: The slate floor makes everyone happy. For Sweetie, it's cool in warm weather; for her humans, it's easy to keep clean.

Linoleum is another floor surface that's easily swabbed, but the tiles should be laid down by someone who knows what he's doing or a lot of mess can gather at the cracks. A good rule of thumb for pet flooring is, the fewer seams, the more high performance the floor. Seamless vinyl flooring is extremely pet friendly, but in the past it's often left a lot to be desired on the aesthetic front. About the only choice available wasn't much of a choice at all: the "look of marble" or a classic black-and-white-checkerboard pattern. Now, however, Armstrong offers a wide range of good-looking patterns, many of them attractive stone-tile look-alikes, plus a patented CleanSweep surface to help keep them looking good.

Another seamless option is terrazzo, a poured cement with chips of marble, glass, or stone that yields a smooth, polished surface. At James Gager and Richard Ferretti's thoroughly modernist apartment, the floors are gleaming white terrazzo that bounces light all over the place. Despite being white, the floor is easy to keep clean with regular mopping and serves as a lovely backdrop for the pitch-black and charcoal gray coats of two standard poodles, Violet and Percy (not to mention the extremely collectible vintage red foam chairs designed by Gae Aulenti for Knoll).

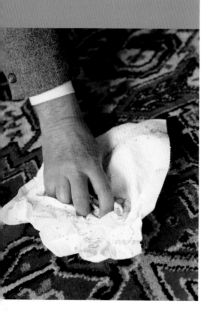

Rare is the animal-house floor with area rugs, and rarer still the animal house carpeted in wall-to-wall broadloom. Besides trapping dust, pet hair, and odors, rugs frequently wind up functioning as sliding surfboards for running pets. In a home with big, active dogs, it takes just moments for rugs to travel long distances. So anchor your rugs or you could see everything in their path come crashing to the floor. (I've seen it happen, which is why I've eliminated rugs from my home.)

Lighter-weight pets, such as cats, won't always displace rugs — but they will have the occasional hairball that usually lands on the most conspicuous place on the rug or carpet. It's one thing if an accident happens at the edge of a rug, making it easier to spot-clean — and quite another when it's right in the middle. If that does happen, clean it up as soon as you notice it, so the unpleasant substance doesn't have time to set in the rug's fibers.

The no-rugs decision is a tough call because obviously if you live anywhere but the ground floor, a rug is needed to muffle the noise of your pets' movements, not to mention your own. In some leases, rugs are a requirement whether you have pets or not. One solution is to look for a rug that's heavy enough not to slide around and to anchor it with a latex nonstick mat and well-placed furniture. Also, it's highly advisable to discourage your pets' running madly about, especially in the middle of the night. The only way to accomplish that is to give dogs quality outdoor exercise time before bedtime, so they're too beat for midnight aerobics.

An excellent carpet compromise is sisal or seagrass. At the home of interior designer and author Sheila Bridges, Dolby the Jack Russell terrier is trained to stay off Sheila's furniture, so the floor is especially important to him. The floor is Dolby's domain, and he has a couple of pet-friendly surfaces to choose from: in the entryway, the original mosaic tilework laid down in 1901, when Sheila's landmark Harlem building was built;

and in the living room, the seagrass rug anchored by sofas and chairs covered in Christopher Norman, Clarence House, and Bennison fabrics. "I'm not a big rug or carpet person," Sheila admits. "The seagrass provides a neutral backdrop that's inexpensive and easily replaced — as opposed to a rare Aubusson!"

Seagrass is tough stuff. It doesn't catch and hold animal hairs and it's very easy to vacuum. Eleanor Mondale covers her living-room floor with a seagrass carpet that withstands hundreds of pounds of quadruped — not to mention the occasional grazing of a miniature horse! "I love seagrass," Eleanor says. "It has a lovely scent, like fresh-cut hay, and it's easy to clean pee and poop out of it with Nature's Miracle." Sisal rugs are great for homes with cats — and indulgent cat people often allow their feline friends to paw at them with impunity, using them as sanctioned scratching surfaces. But sisal does not always stand up well to canines, creating a lot of litter and catching the hairs of long-haired breeds.

Pet lovers who adore wool carpets would sooner invent new ways to live with rugs than sacrifice them altogether. One clever way to enjoy rugs and pets is to display the rugs

Above: Bysshe (named for the poet Shelley) on a rug that never touches the floor: the Turkish sumac Sheri Holman draped over her bedroom chair.

Right: Garbo the Great Dane settles into a George Smith kilim-covered chair.

anywhere *but* on the floor. Sheri Holman has draped a Turkish sumac rug of wool and silk over an armchair in her bedroom; Cathryn Bennion, a dealer in antique textiles, covers her dining table with a splendid old Persian wool carpet. For a more tailored look, there's George Smith's kilim-covered chairs and sofas, which sit just right with Garbo, Anita Monteith's Great Dane.

Charlotte Frieze, *House & Garden*'s garden editor, has great flair when it comes to combining dogs and rugs. Leafing through the *New York Times* one day, Charlotte stopped when she came to an ad for ABC Carpet & Home. The eye-catching image featured a herd of sheep standing on a stunning wool Azari rug. Charlotte figured that carpet could withstand any punishment handed out by her herd of two: the adorably aerobic Airedales Moxie and Rascal. Fortunately, she was right.

Optician and eyewear designer Robert Marc gives his Norfolk terrier Lou Lou the run of his Central Park West spread, the floors of which are notable for their gorgeous antique Oriental carpets. "Those rugs have lived through a lot more than pets," Robert says. "They were dragged through the dirt at some point when they were made, and

they hold up forever — plus, they don't show anything because of their elaborate patterns." The rugs withstand much more than little Lou Lou; a generous host, Robert has frequent get-togethers, and no one has to feel uptight about treading on the carpets.

Rare is the animal house carpeted in wall-to-wall broadloom. Shit happens in an animal house, often on the floor, and carpet cleaning is quite tedious (if you do it yourself) and costly (if you hire professionals). What's more, though you may no longer see or smell evidence of damage, your pet's keen olfactories enable him or her to hone in on the precise spot — and mark it all over again.

Of course, your choice of flooring will be dictated by whether you own or rent. If you rent, work with what you've got; most landlords don't permit changes to their property if they feel those changes won't benefit them in the long run. If you have a reasonable landlord, though, you might try discussing things. If you make the case that you'd like to improve the place at your own expense, and that it would wind up improving the value of your unit for future rentals, he or she might be open to letting you upgrade the carpet, say — or at least change the vinyl flooring from a hideous pattern to a less offensive one, such as black-and-white checkerboard.

If you can't live without wall-to-wall carpeting, select it carefully. Always choose broadloom, not modular tile, as pressure from everyday rough-and-tumble play will cause the edges to lift up much more quickly than expected.

The great news on the flooring front is that new developments in carpet technology are enabling more animal houses to live with carpets stress free. The age-old problem of having pets and wall-to-wall broadloom is that accidents soak through the carpet to the pad underneath, and that's where unpleasant odors stay. But Einstein Moomjy, New York City's ritzy carpet dealer, has turned a lot of customers on to a remarkable new floor covering option. The cutely named Pet-Agree is a polyethylene film backing developed by Solutia. It's laminated directly to the underside of the carpet to keep pet accidents from permeating the padding. Once you've thoroughly cleaned the carpet, you won't have to worry about what lurks beneath it.

Pet-Agree's sole drawback is that currently it's available only on nylon carpet. If you have your heart set on wool carpeting, you'll have to explore other protective options. At Barbara Taylor Bradford's home, the kitchen floors are high-sheen granite, but the sitting room is notable for its wool Stark carpet, which is as snow-white as the coats on Barbara's perfectly groomed bichons frises, Chami and Beaji. Barbara arranged to have a protective process called Fiber-Seal sprayed onto her carpet so that spills bead up for easy blotting. With Fiber-Seal, a technician comes to your home to apply the spray-on coating (the active ingredient of which is a fluoropolymer) directly to upholstered furniture, drapery, and carpeting. It takes several hours to dry. Clients are advised to vacate the premises and to remove pets, especially birds, until the area has been thoroughly ventilated.

More and more, products like Pet-Agree and Fiber-Seal are making it possible for stylish animal lovers to have their carpeting — and enjoy it too.

4.
FOUR WALLS, FOUR PAWS

*E*very animal house must pass a course in Walls 101: what to cover them with.

Textured wallpaper is not a good wall covering for a home with cats, as felines love nothing more than a vertical scratching surface — and what could be more tempting for that purpose than, say, grass-cloth wall covering? But regular, smooth wallpaper can work nicely. In fact, designer Dennis Lee has created several wallpaper patterns in honor of his cocker spaniel, Tyler, who lends his name to Dennis's business, Tyler Hall. Naturally, Dennis's designs are quite popular with animal lovers.

Flat paint has no place in an animal house, period. Pets of all species have a remarkable way of getting stuff on the walls, whether it's food or bodily fluids. Birds love to fling things out of their cages; oils from dogs' coats rub off onto walls, leaving unsightly marks; one shake of a Newfoundland's head, and drool will fly remarkably long distances, landing smack in the middle of the wall. What's more, if a playful dog rolls on her back near a wall, the toenails on her outstretched legs will scratch up the wall beside her (cats often like to paw playfully at walls too). If you've ever tried to clean even the faintest of spots off a wall covered with flat paint, you know that it leaves a scar whose only remedy is repainting.

Semigloss is the highest-performance paint finish to have in an animal house, but think carefully before applying it, as the glaze will throw an unflattering spotlight on any flaws in the plaster of your walls. The more subtle satin or eggshell finish is the decora-

Right: The muse that woofed: Tyler takes a nap at the studio of Dennis Lee, who's in the midst of creating a brand-new wallpaper pattern. Behind Tyler, at right, is the popular Tyler Gardens paper in sage.

Below: The "dog room" at Deborah Hughes's place — deluxe digs or what?

tors' choice because it combines the elegance of flat with the cleanability of gloss. Consult your paint supplier; a seasoned expert will steer you in the right direction. The result will be four walls that stand up admirably to anything your four-legged friends can dish out.

Designer Robert Verdi has created interiors for the likes of Sandra Bernhard, Bobby Flay, and Mariska Hargitay. He recommends that animal houses stick with solid colors straight out of the can, avoiding decorative paint treatments because they're nearly impossible to re-create if you need to cover a trouble spot. Instead of achieving a case of "Out, damned spot," you'll always see where you patched the paint job.

White is a no-brainer color for paint, but there are high-traffic areas in the home where it's simply not practical. Take the entrance to my apartment, where five large, active dogs clamor daily in the vicinity of the front door, whether it's to demand a walk or greet me when I come in. After watching the white walls go prematurely gray in that confined space, I decided to paint the walls and door a more practical color: Cottonwood from Ralph Lauren's Santa Fe collection of paint for Sherwin-Williams.

Bold colors not only look dramatic, they can serve as a wonderful backdrop for pets. Deborah Hughes has designated a room in her home "the dog room" — and it's a showstopper of a space, with brilliant red walls, velvet drapery, a velvet wing chair, and a Biedermeier table. Human visitors see red, but Deborah's Westies only have eyes for the white accent: a Swid Powell cookie jar filled with dog biscuits.

Sometimes animal lovers are moved to use paint that matches the colors of their pets. Sherwin-Williams's Ralph Lauren paint collection includes a lovely shade called Golden Retriever, and no less an authority than Martha Stewart has said that she created several of the elegant colors in her Kmart paint collection by referring to her prized Himalayan cats!

The artist Hunt Slonem hopes someday to start a foundation for unwanted birds. In the meantime, the eight-room, 10,000-square-foot spread in Chelsea where he lives and works is home to the dozens of birds — of all feathers and sizes — he's already taken under his wing (plus one gorgeous Abyssinian cat named Kitu, who never bothers the birds). It's here that Hunt creates the vibrant paintings he's known for; those

Left: In Hunt Slonem's green room, the decor was inspired by the Technicolor plumage of his Amazon parrot, Sybil.

Above and right: At Paul Donaher's Hamptons home, Harry's tack hangs from an antique wrought-iron rack that's a handsome row of horses' heads.

canvases, crowded with delightful images of birds, sell for six figures and up. Hunt's place is a marvel of color, light, and imaginative decoration. No wonder it's one of the stylish set's most sought-after spaces. Fashion designer Tony Melillo of Nova USA, whose clothes are worn by Leonardo DiCaprio and Gwyneth Paltrow, held a recent fashion show there, and photographers have used the premises as a location for shoots of celebrities on the order of Christina Ricci, Tim Robbins, and Gretchen Mol.

Hunt has painted each room a different color; my personal favorite is the green room, which riffs off the dazzling colors of an Amazon parrot named Sybil. Against a chartreuse wall, a vintage sofa upholstered in emerald fabric is piled high with pillows that also complement Sybil's plumage: olive, mustard, and gold. It's a magnificent interior and a fine example of how pets can be a marvelous decorating inspiration. The best part? As it happens, birds love looking at brilliant colors — especially when those colors can be found in their own species' plumage!

After you've settled on paint finish and color, you can turn your attention to what to hang on the walls. If you have one or more dogs, you'll need to designate a portion of one wall for the tack (i.e., all the dog stuff you need for outings, including leashes, collars, training halters, retractable leads, and so forth). Draping leashes on doorknobs or flinging them over chairs is not chic! Styles in tack arrangements can vary from extremely traditional to quite contemporary. Either way, the tack should be ordered neatly and kept that way, so as not to keep a dog with a full bladder waiting while you hunt around for the leash you forgot to hang up properly the night before.

Some people prefer bare walls; others can't live without surrounding themselves with framed artworks. Many animal lovers are collecting animal-themed art *and* living with real, live animals. One who does this with great style is Lisa Fine. Her apartment in Paris is a colorful jewel of an interior, filled with antique furnishings and splendid Indian and Moroccan textiles that Lisa has picked up on her world travels. But the real scene-stealer is artist Joe Andoe's haunting portrait of Malula, Lisa's beloved wheaten terrier. The painting's shaggy inspiration, meanwhile, can usually be found enthroned on the zillion-thread-count Frette linens covering Lisa's bed (for more on that, see chapter 6).

Another dog lover living with two- and three-dimensional canines is the interior designer Stephen Miller Siegel, who shares his home with a pair of irrepressible golden retrievers, Lucy and Harry. On one wall of Stephen's bedroom hangs an impressive collection of framed dog prints that would make Ralph Lauren fans drool, many of

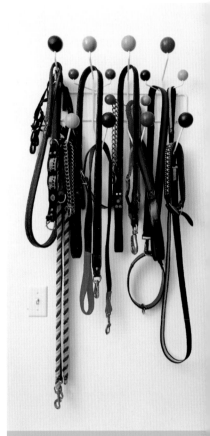

Above: My thoroughly modern pit bulls prefer their tack hanging from an Eames Hang-It-All by Herman Miller.

Below left: *I'm Always with Myself,* part of George Rodrigue's famous "Blue Dog" series, adorns one wall of chef Seen Lippert's home — a tableau made even more vivant by her Shih tzus, Arthur and Buddy.

Below right: Kitty's human is the artist Martha Szabo (a.k.a. my mom). Little wonder this special cat has inspired a gallery of portraits!

Opposite: Backed up by a wall of canine-themed artwork, Lucy looks as serene as a painting herself.

Left: This pack of cast-iron dogs looks almost as expressive as the real thing. But for dog lovers like Stephen Miller Siegel, there's simply no substitute for the living, breathing, genuine article.

them in antique carelian-birch frames; on the floor sits a grouping of highly collectible cast-iron doorstops in the shape of various dog breeds.

Now is certainly an excellent time for collectors of animal-themed art to indulge their pastime. Two of the world's most prestigious auction houses, New York's William Doyle Galleries and London's Bonhams, cohost a joint "Dogs and Cats in Art" sale every February in New York that coincides with the Westminster Kennel Club's annual dog show at Madison Square Garden. On the contemporary art scene, many talented artists are updating the traditional genre of the pet portrait with edgy, often profound

depictions of four-legged creatures, narratives starring pets, or allegorical canvases depicting symbolic animals. The Harry Barker Gallery in Savannah, Georgia, exhibits commissioned oil paintings and sketches of pets. In Brooklyn, New York, there's even a pet artist. Tillamook Cheddar, a.k.a. Tillie, a Jack Russell terrier who lives with the writer Bowman Hastie, creates "drawings" by biting, scratching, and otherwise defacing paper while Bowman videotapes the "artist" at work. If you're thinking, "My pup could've done that," you're absolutely right.

There's no reason our art collections shouldn't please our pets too — remember, decorating an animal house is all about sharing. Interior designer James Fairfax bought a remarkable painting on eBay: It's a vibrant seascape painted by Carlo, the one-name wonder active in Beverly Hills in the 1940s and '50s. Immediately after James placed the highest bid, an unsuccessful counterbidder offered him five times what he paid for it. James resisted, and the painting stays put in his living room, where it gives hours of viewing pleasure to his cat, Silly.

Whether or not your artistic taste runs to animal themes, scale is an issue when it comes to hanging artwork. Murals and large-size canvases can add an unexpected vista to a room. But if you have a male dog who's not completely housebroken, you could wind up heartbroken by urine damage to a favorite artwork. So unless you're certain your dog won't mark indoors, don't hang large-scale artwork where it's in danger of being sprayed by an accidental canine art critic.

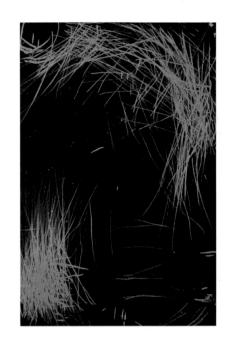

One highlight of Robin Elmslie Osler's loft is the huge, jazzy mural by the artist Steve Keene, a medieval skyline of the German city of Cologne that's a rhapsody in blue and white. Happily, Robin's dogs are extremely well trained — but even if they were to have an accident, the painting would still be safe: Dagmar and Uta are both female, so instead of lifting a leg and aiming at the wall, they'd wet the floor.

Above left: Portrait of the artist as a young dog: Bowman Hastie's creative canine Tillamook Cheddar, a.k.a. Tillie.

Above right: My favorite Tillie "drawing" looks to me like an abstraction of Van Gogh's *Starry Night*.

Left: *Following the Dogs*, Norm Magnusson's allegorical depiction of a racing greyhound.

Strangely, the most pet-friendly artist I've come across isn't renowned for animal portraits. He's Julian Opie, a young Brit whose career is so hot that he recently had *two* concurrent exhibitions at London's prestigious Tate Gallery (one at Tate Modern and another at Tate Britain). So why is he pet friendly? Because he uses a commercial process to create large-scale vinyl "paintings" without paint — his works resemble giant, seamless Colorforms, and they're absolutely gorgeous. They're also proven completely weatherproof, having successfully survived outdoor display. If, say, a male dog decided to express his artistic opinion by lifting a leg near one of these paintings, the artwork would escape completely unscathed.

Creative pet lovers see walls as more than a surface to paint or hang art on. These people look at walls as a wonderful opportunity to integrate their pets' needs with their own.

Many indulgent animal lovers joke that if they're lucky, they'll come back as one of their pampered pets. Well, in my next life — if I have any pull with the reincarnation board — I hope to come back as one of Anna-Sophia Leone's pets. She shares her home with two African gray parrots (Toulouse and Emma), an Amazon (Egon), an umbrella cockatoo (Fiona), and three Norwegian forest cats (Agatha, Claude, and MouChou). Anna-Sophia is one of the gentlest, most caring people I know, and the habitat she's created for her pets is an attractive addition to her well-appointed home. It's so incredibly mindful of their needs — every piece of furniture, every appliance was selected for maximum pet comfort, from the Bionaire air purifiers to the seven-foot-tall cage to the

dust-free Yesterday's News cat litter, made of recycled newspaper — that the animals' contentment is obvious to anyone who spends time with them.

Animal experts strongly caution against trying to establish a peaceable kingdom like this unless you know what you're doing. Anna-Sophia is well versed in the care and maintenance of winged creatures (she's lived in Africa and studied them in their natural habitat, and keeps up with the latest in *Bird Talk* and *The Pet Bird Report* magazines). Beautiful though birds are, they should never be acquired on a whim; caring for them takes hours of work every day, and bird-proofing your home is practically a full-time job. What's more, feathers and fur should never be mixed by anyone who's inexperienced with animals or tragedy could result. (In the case of Anna-Sophia's cats, they are so gentle that the bird-feline combination works out beautifully.)

Watching this happy family hang out in the living room is a special treat. It's hard to imagine upgrading a setup like this, but the perfectionist in Anna-Sophia saw room for improvement. So she hired Sara Lopergolo of G and L Architects to design a state-of-the-art aviary on the south wall of her apartment, complete with two windows, built-in

Left: Robin Elmslie Osler with Dagmar (left), Uta, and the cool vista of Cologne painted by Steve Keene — which, incidentally, looks great with the girls' denim dog beds from L.L. Bean and the heirloom Eames screen.

humidifiers and air purifiers, full-spectrum lighting, screened panels, double-pane glass doors with a soundproofing laminate, and a privacy curtain of velvet with a rubberized backing. When completed, the structure will dovetail perfectly with the architectural details of her landmark prewar apartment building.

By the way, ever since ARQ Architects created the visionary shelter facility Maddie's Pet Adoption Center for the San Francisco SPCA, in which animals live in furnished apartments, the country's most respected master builders are getting accustomed to such requests. (Plans are currently under way for ARQ to redesign the Animal Haven shelter in Queens, New York.) A client recently asked the architect Stephen Learner to design a special area in her home for her dachshund. Like Stephen, David Piscuskas is normally commissioned to create high-end spaces for people. But his firm, 1100 Architect, was not above applying its sleek, modernist aesthetic to Bonnie's K9 Swim Center, a therapeutic exercise pool for injured and handicapped dogs. The result is a deluxe watering hole worthy of a penthouse aerie.

Above: Breakfast time at Anna-Sophia Leone's is as stylish as it is healthy: She eats granola with dried fruit and yogurt from a white Fiesta cereal bowl, while her cats enjoy their food from a matching Fiesta cat bowl.

Right: Taking a dip at Bonnie's K9 Swim Center.

Taking a cue from their exposed brick wall, Gabriele Sanders and Timmy Haskell built a beautiful home for Leeloo, their Moluccan cockatoo. Wrought-iron brackets from Smith & Hawken support Leeloo's stainless-steel bowls and the wooden dowel that

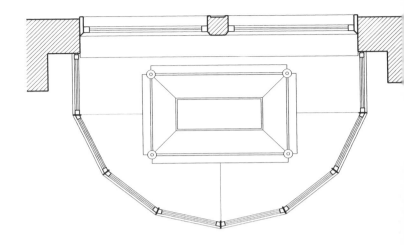

serves as her main perch; higher up hangs a twisty rope perch; and underneath it all is a steel sand trap to collect guano. The result is a beautiful avian environment that looks more like a wall-mounted installation at a trendy art gallery.

Incidentally, birdcages — and our attitude toward them — have come a long way in recent years. Not long ago, cages were approached strictly with an eye to creating things of beauty. The safety of the residents was a very low priority. These days, however, we understand that antique birdcages aren't humane housing for winged pets: They could get their heads stuck in the bars or ingest harmful paint from old wires. So bird lovers buy no-nonsense, epoxy-coated modern cages designed with their birds' needs in mind, and birdcage fanciers collect fanciful antique and reproduction cages, like the splendid examples at ABC Carpet & Home, to use as ornamental accessories that never house a bird. Pottery Barn even markets decorative cages done up as lamps and plant holders — the only correct contemporary functions for ornamental birdcages.

Right: In the stunning star-shaped house that architect Dennis Wedlick designed for the Shah family of upstate New York, a staircase spirals around a birdcage that hangs at the star's center. Visible from several rooms in the home, the cage is quite literally the center of attention!

Below: Gabriele Sanders and Timmy Haskell created this charming habitat for Leeloo, their Moluccan cockatoo.

Observing my felines' affinity for high places, I wondered, why not take advantage of my eleven-foot ceilings to create a vertical feline jungle gym out of shelves designed especially for them? My only aesthetic requirement was that the shelves blend in with the woodwork on my walls, so they'd look as if they belonged there (instead of commanding attention as cutesy kitty playthings, like too many mass-produced items for cats). I consulted on a design with master carpen-

ter Christopher Bailey, who gamely fabricated four architectural wall sconces in the shape of semicircles, each held up by T-shaped wood brackets. Eighteen inches wide and one foot at their deepest, these kitty shelves are big enough for most felines to lie down on comfortably (Christopher sized up the proportions of his own cats just to be sure). For safety, he mounted them to the wall with McFeely's plastic alligators, which, Christopher explains, "mold into" the plaster to support up to sixty-nine pounds. Painted white to match my moldings and arranged in a diamond formation, the sconces look decorative all by themselves — but of course they look much better with a beautiful feline perched on them! And the cats seem to enjoy hopping from shelf to shelf, or just retreating up there for a nap.

One habitat where ornament and function can coexist is the fish tank. It's a carefully controlled ecosystem, yet it's also a living painting — especially when approached with an eye to creating an artful vista on an underwater community. The Delta Society has sponsored studies measuring the calming effect on patients contemplating an aquarium in a dentist's office (where calming effects are sorely needed). People who live with fish are lucky indeed; they can turn to their tanks for immediate stress relief any time of the day or night. And if they're people with a strong aesthetic sense, they'll get even more enjoyment from their tank if it and its setting are easy on the eye.

That's the case at the home of architect Michael Davis, who surrounds himself with beautiful antique furnishings, textiles, and rugs. "They're extremely hypnotic," Michael says of the seventy African cichlids populating the 250-gallon tank in his bedroom, where sunlight streams in through a stained-glass window. "They're wonderful to live with," he adds, "very calming and very lovely." The tank is landscaped with live green anubias plants and earth-toned gravel that coordinates beautifully with the other earth tones in the room. With the fish darting to and fro, the tank brings a soothing aura of vitality to its setting.

Left: Gigi Green and her Devon Rex, Li'l Man, enjoy some elevated aerobics. Clearly architectural cat sconces are an idea whose time has come, and I hope more cat lovers will undertake this simple do-it-yourself project.

Below: How it was done: Christopher Bailey uses McFeely's alligators to anchor the cat sconces to the wall.

People who haven't lived with fish are usually surprised to learn that there's a definite bond between finned pets and the people who maintain their aquatic environments. *New York Post* writer Barbara Hoffman had a real friendship with her late Siamese fighting fish, Goody. He was happy to have Barb pet him every day. "Fish are as observant of you and their surroundings as you are of them," Michael explains. "They really do watch and respond to you. I've had them hide from blond women! They definitely have distinct personalities." If you're lucky, some fish will even swim over to say hello. "I can feed them by hand and they'll let me touch them," he says.

The fish-human bond is reinforced by a restful setting and a good-looking aquarium that enhances the beauty of the creatures swimming inside it. The more beautiful the tank, the more time you'll want to spend contemplating it. That's the credo on which Living Color Enterprises was established. Forget fish tanks — this Fort Lauderdale–based outfit designs, engineers, and fabricates custom architectural *aquarium systems* that lend extraordinary dimension to a wide range of residential and corporate environments. The company reports that more and more homes incorporate aquariums as innovative architectural features in new construction and renovation. Living Color can even match coral to the colors of your decor, or hide unsightly architectural elements (such as a structural steel column) by building a gorgeous aquarium around them, neatly turning eyesores into things of beauty.

Fredrick Fragasso of Fredrick's Aquatic Decor has provided fish tanks for Aretha Franklin, Sean Lennon, and Morley Safer. For marketing and communications executive Stephen Hammond, Fredrick designed an ultramodern, 120-gallon tank of cobalt blue Lucite that would look right at home at Gucci headquarters. Housing thirty-two African cichlids, the tank coordinates swimmingly with Hammond's hip decor, which also incorporates a high-tech Bang & Olufsen stereo system with cobalt blue speakers.

Above: Architect Michael Davis communes daily with the residents of his 250-gallon fish tank.

"I like it when tanks become an integral part of the environment," Fredrick says. "Stephen's apartment is very slick, so that style of tank looks good there. And I always try to re-create the region of the world where the fish come from, whether it's South America, Asia, or Africa. It's trying to take a piece of nature and frame it." Because the cichlids come from the brackish rift lakes of southeast Africa — Lake Tanganyika, Lake Malawi, and Lake Victoria — the aquatic decor incorporates white reef rock and terra-cotta huts for the fish to establish territory in. Those huts, Fredrick explains, "were designed to resemble the kraals built by the Zulus."

What does not belong in a stylish tank? According to Fredrick, "Sunken ships, divers, bubbling monsters, Day-Glo colors . . . There's none of that in my aquariums! Plus, all my fish come from reputable breeders and importers, and go directly to my clients; they never spend time in a pet-shop aquarium, where they could get sick."

Below left: An example of Living Color Enterprises' artistry in a Miami penthouse. The Fort Lauderdale–based company creates exceptional architectural aquariums keyed to your home's decor. Would you believe this gorgeous cylinder conceals a structural steel column?

Below right: Blue heaven: This slick Lucite aquarium, designed by Fredrick's Aquatic Decor, is the ultramodern home of Stephen Hammond's African cichlids.

5.
FETCHING FABRICS

Just last year, the 3M Corporation announced it was discontinuing the production of its world-famous moneymaker Scotchgard. This bold move seemed extraordinarily counterintuitive: a major company turning its back on its own creation, a fabric treatment that had become so synonymous with stain resistance that for some forty years it was routinely recommended for homes with pets. But this was a sign of the times: It seems we'd much rather surround ourselves with materials that require a little more upkeep than live under a protective coating of chemicals.

If 3M's rethinking of Scotchgard sounds counterintuitive, how does having snow-white fabrics in an animal house strike you? The prevailing wisdom has held that when

decorating with pets, we really ought to limit ourselves to a pet-friendly palette of earth tones, sticking with patterns or neutral solids and learning to love all the glorious shades of the color brown. If there's one rule about pet people, though, it's that they make their own rules. It's their house, and they'll do it up white if they want to — even if it means expending extra effort to keep those white interiors clean.

Common sense dictates that if you have pets and you allow them up on the furniture, white is the last color you'd choose. What makes a snowy palette possible in an animal house? Protective slipcovers — and we don't mean the tacky, transparent vinyl kind. The furniture giants — Pottery Barn, Crate & Barrel, Ikea, Ethan Allen — have

Opposite: At the home of handbag designers Richard Lambertson and John Truex, pugs Wallis and Buster share white-slipcovered furniture with a couple of Russian blue cats, Boris and Lily.

changed our collective perception of slipcovers by offering many attractive options in casual and more fitted styles. Pottery Barn's catalog even describes its loose-fit denim slipcovers like this: "Cotton denim covers your sofa so you can eat pizza, sip red wine, or invite the dog up without worry."

More and more, pet lovers swear by washable slipcovers, whether they're off the rack or custom tailored, fashioned of canvas, twill, denim, damask, or chenille. Another advantage to the slipcovered way of life: If your pet has already damaged the sofa, a slipcover can hide a multitude of sins, so you won't have to incur the cost of replacing the entire piece of furniture. No one need know that your sofa isn't brand-new under its nice new clothes!

Eleanor Mondale recently decided to go for a total whiteout after years of living with somber walls and leopard-spotted throws. Suddenly, white just looked right. "My house in Los Angeles was patterned," she explains. "I thought it would be easier with the dogs, so the walls were dark and I had leopard throws covering the couch my dog chewed through while she was still a puppy. I enjoyed the color scheme while I had it, but after a while I got sick of it." Then she moved to New York, where everything looks darker in the absence of the California sun. Jeff Andrews of TFP Design in Los Angeles advised Eleanor to go with white denim. He spoke from firsthand experience, as he'd slipcovered all of his own furniture in white denim to match Ella, the white boxer he rescued.

Right: Staying ahead of shedding requires motivation and frequent sweeping with a vacuum cleaner and/or adhesive hand roller such as Helmac's Tacky Vac. Fortunately, pet hairs are easy to spot against a white slipcover.

"Even people without pets are afraid of white," Jeff says. "They'll say, 'Ooh, white — I can't do *white*.' But I've lived with white slipcovers forever. All you need to do is wash them as often as you have to in hot water and bleach. I'm really into finding good deals in vintage furniture that I recondition and have

reupholstered. But even if I reupholster something in sturdy mohair, I'll still make a white denim slipcover so I have an option." Eleanor was so pleased with her bright new digs, she had two sets of slipcovers made for every piece of furniture she owns. "If they get dirty, they get washed," she says. "It's just like changing your bedding."

I credit my animals with making me a cleaner human being. The fact that white shows dirt is actually an advantage in an animal house — it forces us humans to keep our hygiene level high. "It's frightening to realize how dirty patterned slipcovers can get," Eleanor says with a laugh. "Especially remembering how infrequently I cleaned those

leopard ones! So while dark patterns may cover filth, you wind up sitting down and watching TV in something you really shouldn't be sitting down in. White is way more sanitary when you have pets."

The home Chassie Post and Phil Costello share with their Maltese, Porkchop, and Pomeranian, Stynky, is so attractive it's made the cover of *House Beautiful* magazine. The couple's style is an eclectic blend of vintage thrift-store finds, family heirlooms, and inexpensive new items that grooves with the quirky music of their rock band, Daytona.

Every piece of upholstered furniture is protected by a custom-tailored white canvas slipcover. The slipcovers serve a dual function: Not only do they enable Porkchop and Stynky to romp wherever they please, they unify the otherwise disparate elements of the decor, permitting a Jetsonesque sofa with metal legs to look logical opposite a long, slender 1930s settee.

For those still not sold on white, there are plenty of good-looking patterns for the widest possible range of tastes. The more obvious ones are leopard spots, stripes, plaids, florals, and leaf prints. Or try a fashion-design approach, dressing your home furnishings in hip patterns such as houndstooth, kente cloth, or my favorite, camouflage. Incidentally, camo doesn't have to mean olive drab; there's a jungle full of colors out there, from brilliant blaze orange to leafy Realtree to Urban camo in shades of white, gray, and black. Even though my furniture is covered

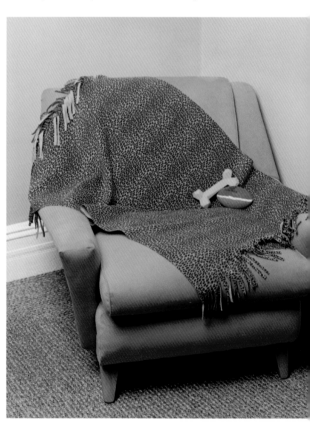

in a high-performance, dog-friendly fabric, when I leave my dogs home alone I still like to apply slipcovers for an added layer of peace of mind. But because my Heywood-Wakefield seats have such an unusual profile, I was obliged to go the more expensive route. Camille Casaretti does precisely such custom work. She made a house call, carefully measured each piece, then whipped up excellent protective slipcovers out of several yards of cotton ripstop fabric in a woodland green camouflage pattern. It's a G.I. Joe/soldier-of-fortune look that really stands up to rough-and-tumble play. My slipcovers are more than just protective layers for when I go out and leave my dogs alone; they're design statements in their own right. Maybe Camille makes such excellent animal-house slipcovers because her cat, a tabby named Calvin (as in Klein), sits in her lap while she sews!

Speaking of fashion designers and furniture, Todd Oldham decided to take an earthy, artisan-couture approach to the ivory slipcovers on his Crate & Barrel loveseat: He prestained them. First he tie-dyed them ocher yellow, then flung inky-blue dye over them in a splatter pattern approximating a Jackson Pollock drip painting. With a pattern like this, you're guaranteed to be ready for almost any type of animal-house accident. "If you don't feel like dyeing the fabric yourself," Todd suggests, "ask the vendors at your local flea market if they know anyone who makes tie-dye T-shirts, and talk to them about doing it for you."

Even more than color or pattern, durability and longevity are important factors to consider when selecting fabrics for your animal house. Besides being easy on the eye and cool to the touch, linen is one of the world's sturdiest natural fibers. As interior designer Robert Verdi likes to say, "Remember, mummies were wrapped in linen for centuries — and they survived." In the case of slipcovers, linen also happens to launder beautifully. Robert Marc's furniture is upholstered in a very practical solid linen from Rogers & Goffigon; the color's name is, literally, Mud. Still, he's not taking any chances: He regularly has his upholstered furniture treated with the Fiber-Seal process.

The Finnish textile firm Marimekko is world famous for vibrant, dynamic patterns as exuberant as a romp in the dog run. I've been eyeing some of their gorgeous heavyweight linens for my animal house, especially the navy-and-gray Aato, with its freestyle fruit-bowl motif, and the burgundy Runo, adorned with leafy vines in gold or silver.

Below: Ann, Todd, and the splatter-patterned sofa Todd designed to camouflage "any pet problems that might occur."

81

Above: In Robert Marc's living room, Lou Lou is welcome absolutely anywhere, thanks in part to a Rogers & Goffigon linen upholstery fabric whose name is Mud.

If you enjoy populating your home with images of critters, and animal-themed wallpaper and artwork aren't enough, Lee Jofa offers a range of animal-themed printed fabrics by G.P. & J. Baker. Available in cotton chintz or linen, these feature such amusing patterns as Pugs and Petals, Whippets, and Directoire Parrot. While chintz is fine for very small pets (i.e., lap breeds), stick with linen if you plan to let larger animals sit on anything upholstered in these lovely patterns. Take it from one who's tried living with chintz and big dogs: "I don't recommend chintz unless it's for a throw pillow," says Eleanor Mondale. "You can't wash or dry it, and it just doesn't look the same after repeated dry-cleanings. Believe me, you can live stylishly without chintz!"

For a pristine modern look, Maharam creates extraordinary fabrics that are nothing less than upholstery artworks. And no wonder: They're based on original designs by twentieth-century giants like Ray and Charles Eames, George Nelson, Alexander Girard, and Werner Panton. Barring the black-and-white patterns, many of these are surprisingly forgiving of pet stains.

For a home with cats, it's best to stick with smooth surfaces, including (believe it or not) velvet. Most of us think of velvet as one of the most fragile of fabrics. But Saint Francis de Sales (the patron saint of journalists and writers) said, "Nothing is so strong as gentleness" — and that's especially true with regard to this regal textile. Many cats simply aren't interested in velvet because their claws glide along it too easily and they prefer more of a challenge! What's key is selecting your velvet with an eye to normal animal activity. Anna-Sophia Leone bought a Laura Ashley sofa covered in slub velvet. The fabric starts out with built-in flaws, and further distressing from her three cats and

four birds only enhances its rich, antique appearance. Good ol' cotton can also be quite durable. Charlotte Frieze recently replaced the fabric on her sofa and loveseat with the same Clarence House Bristol cotton she used to upholster the pieces the first time around — fifteen years ago. For an animal house, that's a very decent track record.

As for me, I can't say enough good things about Ultrasuede, which is why I've covered my early-1950s Heywood-Wakefield sofa and chairs in the stuff, and even had Ultrasuede dog and

Left: At the home of Arden and Daryl Dewbrey, durable cotton fabrics by Cowtan & Tout permit Dagny the beagle to be more than a couch potato — she's a regular sofa sporting hound!

Below left: Pepper on the Heywood-Wakefield chair upholstered to match her coat. She blends in so well with the ginger Ultrasuede that I've seriously considered renaming her. (Ludmilla the cat is a chic shade of gray that blends with everything!)

Below right: Britannia Tige luxuriates on Hide Ultrasuede. The double portrait of my white dog Daisy was painted by Daisy's grandmother, Martha Szabo.

cat beds made. I'm indebted to Toray Industries for turning me on to the extreme pet friendliness of its proprietary polyester microfiber. Generally speaking, fashion arbiters tend to shun anything made of polyester, but they're happy to make an exception for Ultrasuede, which has turned up in the hip and happening collections of Stephen di Geronimo and Anna Sui. Ultrasuede looks and feels like real suede, yet no animals are sacrificed for its manufacture. It's also machine washable, spot cleanable with soap and water, highly resistant to odors, and always stays cool and comfortable to the touch in any climate — all important virtues in an animal house.

What's more, Ultrasuede looks right on a wide variety of furniture styles, from traditional to midcentury modern to futuristic (De Sede's electric recliner, which is *Blade Runner* meets Archie Bunker). The next time I redecorate, I'm going with Willie Landels's sleek Throw-Away collection of furniture (two- and three-seat sofa, armchair, and pouf), designed in 1965 and still produced by the Milanese firm Zanotta. The upholstery stretches over an expanded polyurethane frameless body, attaches with Velcro, and is completely removable for washing. Naturally, I'd have it covered in (what else?) Ultrasuede.

With traditional woven fabrics, pet hairs — particularly the hairs of short-coated dogs like mine — work their way into the weave like stubborn little quills. Ultrasuede is a microfiber, which means that it's created by squishing together millions of filaments so thin they're practically invisible. There's no way pet hairs, even my dogs' needlelike ones, can penetrate a barrier like that. And so the hairs stay on the surface, where they're easily vacuumed up or lifted with tape rollers. Still, I keyed the color of my Ultrasuede furniture to my dogs' coats on the theory that the hairs would be less noticeable between sweepings if they blended in with the upholstery. The armchair was matched to my buckskin dog, Pepper; the sectional sofa is an earthy shade of brown to coordinate with the brown-and-black markings of my brindle, Britannia Tige.

Harold Koda, curator of the Costume Institute at the Metropolitan Museum of Art in New York, knows a great deal about stylish textiles; he also shares his home with two adorable Chinese crested dogs, Lapsang and Souchong (Lapsy and Souchy for short). For the sofa, chairs, and ottoman in his living room, Harold selected a mohair by Old World Weavers. "It's very durable," he says. "The girls nest and claw away at it, but I don't have to worry about it. If it was silk damask, you'd just be crazed." Lapsy and Souchy are hairless but for their heads, legs, and tails. Still, Harold points out, "what little hair they have sheds quite a lot, so selecting the color of the fabric became an issue of what wouldn't show all those long, blond strands." Accordingly, he opted for a golden-tan shade that happens to be the exact same color as the golden highlights in the girls' bombshell-platinum fur patches — and, snuggling together on the ottoman, Lapsy and Souchy certainly look like a couple of glamorous Jean Harlows.

The textile industry uses something called the Wyzenbeek test to determine how upholstery fabrics stand up to everyday friction caused by our clothes. During this test, a fabric sample is subjected to an abrasive material clamped on an oscillating drum

Above: Lapsang and Souchong, Harold Koda's Chinese cresteds, naturally gravitate toward an ottoman covered in a sturdy golden-tan mohair that matches the golden highlights in their fur.

Right: Leather sofas provide a cozy, durable nest for Amy Kizer's Shiba inus, Lucy and Tonto.

operating at the rate of ninety double oscillations (or double rubs) per minute. The evaluation criterion is the minimum number of double rubs that produces a variation in the color, gloss, or appearance of the finished surface. It so happens that Ultrasuede surpasses 200,000 Wyzenbeek double rubs. But never mind that — more important, this miracle fabric withstands daily punishment from my aerobic crew of pit bulls, yet still manages to look brand-new. Ultrasuede is great for cats too, because its smooth surface either proves uninteresting to the average feline claw or tough enough to survive scratching. My mother's woven-wool dining chairs took a serious beating from her industrious cats. Since the same chairs were re-covered in Ultrasuede, the kitties no longer bother with them (or if they do, they leave no evidence behind).

Believe it or not, there are fabrics that surpass even Ultrasuede when submitted to the Wyzenbeek test. One of these is chenille cord by Maharam, a 100 percent solution-dyed nylon that exceeds one million double rubs. This is the material I selected to cover the cushion my dogs sit, stand, and jump on by their favorite window. For furnishings where a little more tenderness is in order — i.e., cocooning hot-spots like the sofa — there's Maharam Scout, a 100 percent polyester chenille with a Teflon finish that's as velvet soft as it is strong.

I recently had dog bed covers made out of another Maharam contract textile called Simulate, which is made of polyurethane bonded to a polyester knit. The dogs love these NASA-style beds done up in space-age colors like orange and silver — and I love the fact that water, drool, and other liquids roll right off them. Interior designer Jeffrey Bilhuber's favorite pet-friendly textile is a woven Teflon made by Larsen. "It's an extraordinary material because it looks like silk taffeta," Jeffrey explains, "but you can pour anything on it — chocolate syrup, toxic waste — and it'll just bead right up." Too bad scratchy woven Teflon isn't the most inviting surface for pets.

Then again, for some people, outsmarting pets by means of shrewd fabric choice is the whole point. After one of her dogs shredded the sofa, actress Bernadette Peters told me she planned to re-cover it in Sunbrella, a weather-resistant fabric designed for outdoor furniture upholstery. "But," I protested, "your dogs won't like the way it feels." Bernadette just chuckled with that beautiful, Tony Award–winning voice of hers. "I know," she replied — and I swear you could hear her wink.

If you opt not to use a high-performance microfiber like Ultrasuede, or a fabric with a Teflon finish, or some other high-tech textile, be sure that the material you select for your upholstery has a tight weave — or opt for fabrics that aren't fabrics at all: leather or vinyl, which is high-performance by any name, whether it's called pleather or leatherette. Many animal lovers gravitate toward synthetic leather because it's cruelty free and 1970s hip, but people who don't mind using genuine leather in their interiors quickly discover that it's almost as easy care as vinyl, and pets prefer the way it feels to its imitators, which can get hot and sticky. If, however, your dog also loves the way leather tastes, you could have a problem. Alas, one of my dogs (who shall go nameless) took just a few hours to demolish an entire seven-foot-long leather sofa and was just getting started on the last surviving cushion by the time I walked in the door. That's why I switched to Ultrasuede, which doesn't seem to taste as good as it looks.

Above: Cyrus gets comfortable on a Coach leather chair, which happens to highlight his orange eyes.

Yet there are many animal houses where a leather sofa is not an endangered species. Michael Levinson deliberately selected grade-three leather for his living-room sofa because, he explains, "leather is easy to wipe clean and it looks better with age." Television producer Glenn Davish bought a leather sofa so his beagle, Gertie, would stay cool while lounging there in the summer. Many makers of contemporary furniture are rolling out compelling styles, from Ethan Allen and Pottery Barn to pricier models by Maurice Villency and Roche-Bobois. Minotti offers hip, handsome couches made of leather accented with calf hide. The latter is highly efficient at hiding dog and cat hairs because it's hairy by nature itself; for the same reason, plush faux-fur throws are also popular with pet lovers, whether they're inexpensive (like Bed, Bath & Beyond's deep-brown "mink") or very high end (Takashimaya's deluxe beige throw, a favorite of Oprah Winfrey's). Yet antique leather also has undeniable charm. The scores of vintage leather sofas and chairs at New York's ABC Carpet & Home are testament to leather's enduring appeal and staying power, as are the funky 1960s leather sofa beds at the home of Amy Kizer, whose company, Wagwear, supplies collars and raincoats to dog walkers with names like Rupert Everett and Courteney Cox.

The leather-goods giant Coach has a line of home furnishings upholstered in a variety of hides; for animal houses, the company recommends thick, heavy-grain leather in brown, rather than glove-soft black napa, which is more prone to showing signs of wear and tear (especially in a home with cats). De Sede makes some of the most beautiful leather furniture in the world; it's also some of the most pet-proof, as it's upholstered in heavy-duty, dark brown neck hide that's extremely scar resistant.

The only absolute no-no materials for an animal house are any kind of silk and irreplaceable antique textiles. Woven wool is not recommended either, as our pets' claws can get caught in it, resulting in unsightly upholstery snags. Museum of Modern Art curator Paola Antonelli is recognized the world over as the high priestess of contemporary design and sought out for her opinions on everything from fashion to folding chairs. I couldn't resist asking Paola to weigh in on the subject of animal-house style. Well, it turns out my esteemed curator friend's demanding job prevents her from having pets. So, not surprisingly, she offered some unimpeachably practical advice: Avoid inflatable PVC, such as the kind used on the iconic Blow armchair first created in 1967, or its direct descendant, Ikea's award-winning Air collection of inflatable furnishings. Obviously, one claw puncture and your air-filled furniture has had it.

Then again, what did we say about pet lovers breaking the rules and making their own? With all due respect to Paola, I noticed that the catalog for Zanotta, the company that manufactures the Blow chair, features an adorable Boston terrier sitting proudly on one of these inflatable wonders. Jean-Claude Huon, meanwhile, has a drop-dead-gorgeous sofa by B&B Italia that's covered in ivory woven wool, of all things. Zulla, his cat, has already left a few scratch marks in one spot at the side — but Jean-Claude just shrugs and smiles. Talk about counterintuitive fabric choices — and a live-and-let-live lifestyle!

Left: In its catalog, Zanotta demonstrates an animal-house sensibility by featuring this photograph of its iconic Blow chair alongside the caption, "Every creature is defined by its environment. Even a dog needs a place to settle down."

6.
WHOSE BED IS IT, ANYWAY?

*W*hen we really like someone, we do our best to spend the night with him or her. Pet people are no exception. Our love for animals is obvious in the elaborate sleeping arrangements we make for our pets.

Some breeds demand mattress rights more than others. Dachshunds — a.k.a. "wiener dogs" — are champion cocooners. "They absolutely insist on sleeping in bed with you," says Adrian Milton, founder of a breed-appreciation group called the Dachshund Friendship Club. "And when they get into bed, they'll pull the covers right up over themselves." Getting them into bed, however, is another story.

It's not that they're playing hard to get; the breed's short legs make it impossible for them to get onto a bed without a little help. And once they're up there, heaven forbid they should suddenly be overcome with the desire to jump down, as they could severely injure their elongated spines. Ellie Cullman, principal in the interior-design firm of Cullman & Kravis, recalls with a giggle how one client requested that a special set of mahogany bedside steps be built to enable her dachshund to reach her nineteenth-century four-poster mahogany bed, which stood twenty-seven inches off the ground. "The steps were beautifully done," Ellie says, "with wood turnings to coordinate with the posts on the bed."

Of all the plush places in her mistress's beautifully appointed town house, Faith Popcorn's Japanese chin, Miyake (who's named for the visionary avant-garde Japanese fashion designer Issey Miyake), prefers the bedroom's nineteenth-century wrought-iron

Opposite: Interior designer Robin Bell Schaefer with her two foxy dachsies: the long-haired Schnitzel (left) and the wire-haired Thumper.

canopy bed. Seeing as the bed is dressed in Frette sheets and accessorized with lavender-filled organic-cotton pillows, who can blame her? But like our dachshund friends, Miyake can't reach her favorite spot on her own. Faith is a bestselling author, trend-forecasting guru, and founder of the marketing firm BrainReserve, so it was a no-brainer for her to devise a brilliant plan: have a step custom-built and -upholstered to coordinate with the other furnishings in her bedroom. It's an elegant solution that frees Miyake to come and go as she pleases.

Fancy accoutrements and spooning aside, what our pets love best about our beds is those posture-friendly mattresses. Responding to the reality that all dogs would love a mattress of their own, Matthew Morris of Blue Ribbon Dog Company created the stain-resistant Red Rover dog bed, which looks for all the world like a mini Serta, circa 1940s, complete with removable striped covers meant to evoke mattress ticking. To whet canines' appetites for deluxe bedding — especially channel-stitched down quilts — he came up with the extremely durable K9 Sport dog bed, baffled to hold the filling in place so it won't flatten out like a pancake.

Christopher Brosius, founder of the hip Demeter Fragrance Library, learned about his dog's appetite for bedding the hard way, after he made a simple bed for himself, putting a $1,500 king-size Sealy Posturepedic mattress directly on the floor of his bedroom. One evening while Christopher went out to dinner, his mastiff, Zephyr, went to work. "By the time I got home two hours later, he had totally ripped the bed to pieces," Christopher recalls. "There were feathers everywhere, and all the bedding was destroyed, including the brand-new camel-hair blanket I'd just gotten at a good price, and the really nice Egyptian cotton sheets I'd bought at the Bloomingdale's white sale." As for the mattress? "He peeled the top off like it was a tin of sardines. There were springs and bits of rubber everywhere."

Above: Miyake is a pea-sized princess in Faith Popcorn's stately canopy bed.

Right: Easy does it: the custom-upholstered step that helps Miyake reach her goal.

Opposite: André and Christian are named after two giants of twentieth-century design, André Courrèges and Christian Dior. The Italian greyhounds certainly look like designer dogs on their K9 Sport bed.

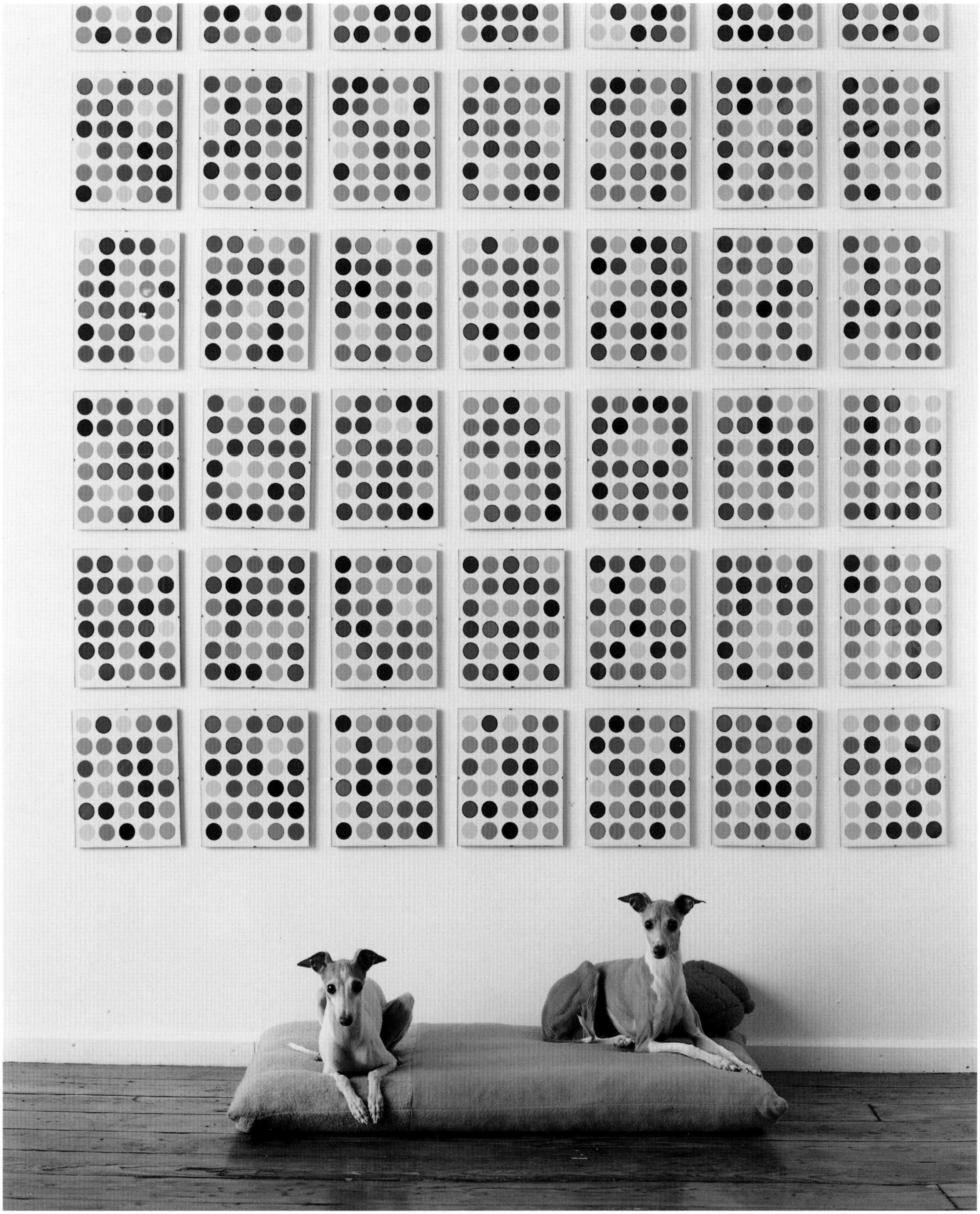

Below left: Zephyr rests easy on the king-size Sealy Posturepedic "dog bed" that survived a two-hour chewing session.

Below right: Woofer hogs the water bed, which is protected by a durable, washable Vellux cover.

Fortunately, Christopher was able to repair the mattress with duct tape, flip it over, and continue sleeping on it. Since then, however, his taste in bedding has changed. "It was a really elaborate bed; it's much simpler now," Christopher says. Dressed these days in handsome heavy-duty brocade fabrics, the bed is still Zephyr's favorite place to catch some Zs.

It's a little-known subset of Murphy's Law that a lot of unfortunate animal-house accidents happen in bed, especially vomiting and hair-ball spitting (some pets, feeling regurgitation coming on, will somehow manage to make it up onto the bed from all the way across the room just in time to create a spectacular mess). You can flip a soiled mattress only so many times, so if you do allow your pets on the bed, invest in a good, thick mattress pad and several sets of cotton sheets, plus at least one washable duvet cover. For puppies or older dogs, you may want to rig the mattress with a protective vinyl cover or vinyl tablecloth (or just keep the bedroom door closed while you're out).

The style and color of your sheets are entirely up to you (so long as you avoid black, which shows more than anyone wants to see). Many pet lovers go for a dark, patterned effect. One of the most popular sheets in the dog-loving world is Ralph Lauren's Aragon, a leopard-patterned set endorsed by supermodel Veronica Webb, who shares

her spotted bed with a dachshund named Hercules. Ikea also has wonderful sheets in dark, abstract patterns that are quite forgiving of pet hair and dirt. But to my surprise, I found that many pet owners are, in the words of Stephen Miller Siegel, "white-sheet fanatics," including Stephen himself, who favors linens by Frette. And yet, his golden retrievers are more than welcome on Stephen's bed, which stays miraculously clean. The trick? Vintage linens. Stephen collects these frayed, torn, holey, monogrammed examples of bedding past and throws them over his duvet to protect it. For the same purpose, Kohle Yohannan uses an inexpensive gray blanket from Target that's made of high-performance, easy-care Vellux (nylon embedded in a reinforced urethane layer to form a pile on both sides). Following his lead, I recently bought my pit bulls a good-looking Martha Stewart Everyday Vellux blanket at Kmart.

As for bedspreads, shams, and coverlets, matelassé fabric turns out to be as durable as it is decorative; the tight quilting defies jumping paws and repeated washings. Matelassé is available in a wide range of patterns and price points everywhere from The Company Store and Kmart to Chambers and Garnet Hill. At the very high end, Troy, the home-furnishings store in New York's SoHo, offers a keen solution for bed-bound pet lovers. Their sleeping bag is camel-colored Ultrasuede on the outside and charcoal gray cashmere on the in — and it zips open to form the ideal pet-friendly duvet. The opulent cashmere side touches you; the equally opulent yet eminently washable Ultrasuede side is your pet's. Brilliant!

As for the style of your bed itself, steer clear of upholstered headboards, or select one with a headboard covered or slipcovered in performance fabrics, such as the Pascal Mourgue bed from Ligne Roset. Flou makes a wonderful bed called the Nathalie that's high on my list of objects to acquire: It's got a tough steel frame that's sure to support the weight of several large dogs; it's upholstered in cotton canvas or Ultrasuede (guess which one I'll be getting?), which means nighttime dog drool, not to mention human drool, sponges right out; the pillow shams tie to the headboard; and the slatted frame holding the mattress lifts up for easy linen storage, a blissful bonus in an animal house with limited space. Even more practical is any style of wrought-iron bed, popular for centuries because the absence of crevices means they're easy to keep clean and bed-bug free.

Above: Chez Lisa Fine, plain white sheets protect the Frette linens from paw prints, so Malula the wheaten terrier is always welcome on Lisa's splendid bed (check out the embroidered headboard Lisa designed, inspired by the gorgeous temples of Jaisalmer in Rajasthan).

After years of waking up with limbs numbed from several heavy dogs resting their heads on my legs and arms all night, I have been tempted many times to build a high loft bed with retractable steps, so the dogs could sleep *under* my bed (and I could retain some circulation). But I never get around to that because I love sleeping with my animals too much — especially in deep winter, when they prove quite thermally efficient. Apparently, I'm not alone. Interior designer Jeffrey Bilhuber has created interiors for the likes of Iman and David Bowie. Not long ago, Jeffrey accommodated a dog-loving client by designing a special ten-foot-long bed so the man could sleep comfortably with his family of pugs, who reserve the right to romp down at the foot of the bed. At forty inches wide, the bed is slightly roomier than a twin, yet not wide enough for two people. It's upholstered in sand Indian ribbed cotton (to coordinate with the pugs' sandy coats) and features sturdy bronze legs.

Even two tiny toy dogs in bed can severely cramp your style, as *Worth* magazine publisher Randall Jones and his wife, Connie, discovered after spending many sleepless nights with their two Shih tzus, Blitz and General Lee. The couple devised an ingenious solution that extends the length of their king-size bed. They simply pulled a caned chaise, covered in the same yellow chintz used for the bedspread, up to the foot of the mattress. An added bonus: The wraparound arm on the chaise ensures that the girls won't fall off in the middle of the night.

Other pet lovers are made of tougher stuff, so they make deals with their four-legged roommates, sometimes resorting to outsmarting tactics to designate and preserve no-paws zones. As we saw in chapter 2, Han Feng is remarkably laid-back about her Hoffmann table and chairs. Her bed, however, is a different story. She doesn't mind sharing it with her housebound cats, but like many urban dwellers, she'd rather keep her bed linens clear of canine paws that tread the mean city streets. So she designed a special bed of unfinished pine that's way too high for Lulu, her beagle, to reach (in fact, Han herself needs a bamboo footstool to get up there). But the cats, José and Babé, have no problem gaining access whenever they feel so inclined. (Don't feel too bad for Lulu: She's got her own comfy cushion right under her mistress's bed.)

Left: Han Feng on the bed she had custom built to outsmart her beagle, Lulu.

Joe Dolce keeps his bedroom a no-paws zone with the help of a sliding pocket door that his brainy pups haven't figured out how to open (yet). Sheila Bridges carries her strict no-dogs-on-the-furniture policy all the way to her bedroom — but, recognizing pets' need to sleep near us even if that means on the floor, she's graciously placed her dog's bed on the bedroom floor. Gabriele Sanders has ruled her mosquito-netted platform bed off-limits to her dogs. The cats, however, are always welcome. With felines, the bed becomes a wonderful playground — especially when it's time to make it. My cats love to prolong the bed-making process, turning it into a game by pouncing on unfurling sheets and wiggling around under the covers.

For people who choose to live with pets despite persistent allergies, or for a household in which one family member is allergic, doctors recommend that the allergic person's bedroom be ruled off-limits at all times; the pet shouldn't even be allowed to walk in there.

Whether or not your pets are your bedmates, providing them with their own nest to sleep in is a good idea. That way, there's a place in the animal house that's theirs and theirs alone — like the Gucci dog bed beloved by my Britannia Tige. As wonderful as it is, there's one critical problem with that item: It's been discontinued.

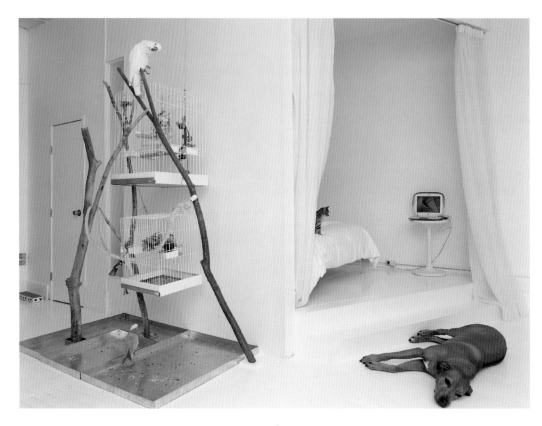

Kathy Bishop can appreciate iconic home furnishings; her home might as well be a gallery of modernist furniture design, with its white walls, Edward Fields rug, Paul McCobb coffee table, and Eero Saarinen marble-top table and Womb chair. Faced with the worldwide shortage of Gucci Lucite dog beds, she and her husband, Jim Rosenthal, came up with a solution that saved them some money. Inventing their own homage to modernist canine design, they designed a Plexiglas dog bed, had it fabricated by a company called Plexi-Craft, and rigged it with a foam cushion covered in interchangeable Ultrasuede slipcovers, one in sunny yellow and the other in royal blue (to match the blue Womb chair). Kathy wittily dubbed their creation the "No-Gucci" dog bed — and the name stuck.

The Gucci dog bed is in my opinion the poshest in history — with the exception of the splendid velvet kennel custom-built for Marie Antoinette's tiny Continental spaniel, a cousin of the papillon. History books gloss over what happened to the resident of that little kennel after his queen was taken to the gallows. But the kennel itself survives in New York's Metropolitan Museum of Art as proof of just how far some of us will go to make our pets comfortable.

Above left: Echoes of Mies Van der Rohe: German architect Philipp Plein created this bed for his dog. Faux fur is just one upholstery option!

Above right: Billy gets down to business on his "No-Gucci" dog bed with built-in storage area for toys.

Left: Marie Antoinette's toy spaniel slept in this velvet-covered dog kennel, which now resides in the Metropolitan Museum of Art.

Today's dog owners show how much they care by creating equally luxe nests for their sleepy friends. "When she's not sleeping on my bed, this is a nice replacement," says Oprah Winfrey of the circular down-filled dog bed she bought from The Company Store (and had monogrammed!) for her adorable pup Sophie. Interior designer Michael Levinson, who collects splendid early-nineteenth-century American Empire furniture, even designated a narrow sofa with lion's-paw feet as the "dog bed" for his Lab mix, Murray, who's never so much as been tempted to leave tooth marks on the sofa's ornate wood carvings. When reupholstering it became inevitable (the wool fabric on it had grown "quite stinky," Michael reports), Michael feared that "Murray would be mad at me for removing his sofa" — so he arranged an upholsterer's house call. That way, Murray and his dog bed weren't separated for long, and he didn't miss it a minute longer than necessary. As covered in African Leopard Ultrasuede, the bed won't need redoing for a very long time, because the microfiber resists odors and the spotted pattern is quite forgiving of stains.

That's not Murray's only sleeping arrangement, however. He also has access to Michael's bed, which is routinely dressed in pricy 430-thread-count sheets. The mattress is about six inches lower than normal, a concession to Murray's advanced age. Sleep studies have proven just how active we humans are in our sleep, but that's nothing compared to Murray's nocturnal movements. "He'll sleep on the bed . . . then he'll go to his sofa . . . then he'll move on to the sofa in the living room," Michael says. "I usually wake up in the morning and find him on his bed. But sometimes I'll wake up and find him on mine!"

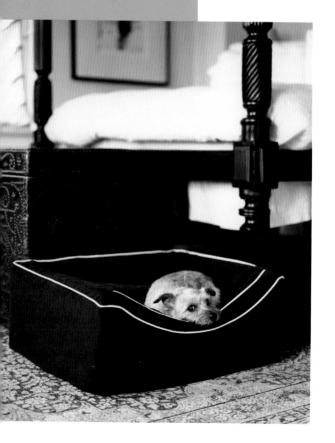

Above: Morgen is getting slee-e-eepy on her girlie wicker dog bed.

Below left: Lou Lou looks as if she'd like some privacy, please!

Below right: Within seconds of curling up in their beds, Blaze (left) and Monroe are down for the count. You would be too if your bed looked as dreamy as a Krispy Kreme donut.

There's a style of dog bed out there to suit every dog person's aesthetic. Deborah Hughes's Westies, Morgen and Romy, sleep in charmingly girlie wicker baskets lined with Provençal fabrics and beribboned cushions. Robert Marc's Norfolk terrier, Lou Lou, on the other hand, goes for a more tailored look with a navy dog bed trimmed in white piping that's parked at the foot of the master bedroom's handsome colonial-style four-poster. Benito and Bess, George Malkemus and Tony Yurgaitis's pair of Scotties, whose portraits have been painted many times by shoe-designer-to-the-stars Manolo Blahnik, prefer their beds in the shape of, well, dogs (complete with long, floppy, monogrammed ears).

As long as it's comfy and protects weary joints from the cold, hard floor, a dog bed needn't be ultrahaute or ultracute; it needn't even be a bed *per se.* Ikea markets a plush, machine-washable white sheepskin throw that makes a wonderful dog nest (provided your dogs don't love to shred sheepskin, as mine do). The architect-designer Clodagh lives with Van Gogh (nickname: Van Dog), a twenty-three-year-old German shepherd mix so named because of the divot on his ear that was there when Clodagh found him nineteen years ago, emaciated and shivering on the street. I suspect Van's years have earned him a mention in *The Guinness Book of World Records,* and by now he's quite

Left: Clodagh and Van Gogh, whose moving blanket is never out of reach.

Below: Benito and Bess like their dog-eared beds monogrammed.

stiff in the joints. Although he's more than welcome on the furniture, he's physically unable to get up there. So Clodagh makes sure to have Van's favorite quilted moving blanket available for him whenever and wherever he decides to lie down for the evening. Of course, because Clodagh is so design conscious, that blanket happens to be the chicest these eyes have ever seen, in black with tan piping!

7.
SOMEONE'S IN THE KITCHEN WITH FIDO

The kitchen leads a double life. It's the most popular room in the house, the place where everyone congregates at parties because delicious meals are prepared there. But it's also one of the more hazardous rooms, because the concentration of sharp objects and hot surfaces makes it the site of so many accidents. The kitchen can be especially hazardous to pets, so certain precautions should be taken toward avoiding emergency trips to the vet.

Our homes are so important to us that deluxe kitchen appliances have assumed the cachet once reserved for expensive cars and speedboats. It seems no stylish home is without its Sub-Zero refrigerator. I know a woman whose dog opened her refrigerator and ate just about everything inside it. One advantage of the Sub-Zero for an animal house is that it's not very easy to open, even for some humans! The slick-looking Viking stove is the Rolls-Royce of ranges — no wonder it's become a bona fide millennial status symbol. But the Viking also gives off a lot of heat, so animals should be kept far from the kitchen during operation, or closely supervised by someone other than the busy cook.

Even if you haven't got a megarange, it's best to have someone else supervise the pets when you're in full-throttle culinary mode, especially if you're trying to keep pace with Emeril Lagasse each time he kicks it up a notch. "Ibrahim is never allowed to be on her own in the kitchen," says novelist Sheri Holman of her beloved mustache parakeet. "If we're boiling water or making dinner, one of us will do the cooking and the other will

keep watch over the bird." Sheri jokes that making a home safe for animals is excellent training for kid-proofing. "If we decide to have a baby, it'll be a piece of cake!" she says.

If you're cooking and preparing food alone, keep pets out of the kitchen, especially small, fast-moving, nimble, curious ones such as cats, ferrets, and rabbits. Between juggling open flames, boiling water, and chopping knives, you won't be able to watch your pets vigilantly, and too many mishaps can occur. And for obvious reasons, fancy knife sets hanging from a magnetized strip on the wall have no place in an animal house.

When you're not using the kitchen to cook, stash dish-washing detergents and soapy sponges in the under-sink cabinet (cats often like to pick apart sponges with their teeth, and dish-washing liquid is the last thing they need to add to their diets). Also, make sure not to leave sharp objects, such as food-processor blades, lying about in the dish rack. See? In addition to making us cleaner people, our pets, if well cared for, can also make us better organized. Despite the more obvious hazards of the average kitchen, some pets find a safe nesting place there. Nothing's sweeter than the sight of Anna-Sophia Leone's cat MouChou curled up in a bread basket on the counter!

Invisible dangers that can be equally harmful to pets, if not more so, also lurk in the kitchen. When used at high temperatures, some nonstick coatings may emit a fume that can be harmful—even deadly—to birds, so bird lovers must take care not to use nonstick cookware around birds. Some modern ovens incorporate nonstick parts, so check with the manufacturer before buying or using an oven you're not sure about.

For bird people, retro appliances have even more cachet than their high-tech contemporary counterparts. When Sheri Holman purchased her home, she was especially thrilled about the 1950s hooded South Bend range. It made the job of bird-proofing her new home for Ibrahim that much simpler. Kohle Yohannan cooks in a textbook example of a bird-safe kitchen. After falling hard for a 1936 steel-and-

red-enamel Electrolux vacuum cleaner, he went for a heavy-metal look in his kitchen, the walls of which are lined in galvanized tin and fitted with red-enameled hardware-store cabinets (on top of which sits the Electrolux machine that inspired the decor). Except for the brand-new fridge, every appliance is a piece of history, from the stainless laboratory sink to the 1950s stove to the 1950s General Electric oven that's set into the wall. And since these appliances were manufactured before the 1960s, when nonstick finishes began to be applied to cooking surfaces, they're safe to use in the presence of Kohle's sulphur-crested cockatoo, Tweeter, whose cage is set up in the kitchen.

However you set up your pantry, all food should be stored well out of reach of curious paws and claws, on high shelves or behind cabinet doors. A clever pet can get into things he's not meant to ingest and get quite sick to his stomach. One evening, I brought home a decadent ricotta cheesecake, cut off a slice, set it out on a plate with a fork perched on the plate's edge, and went to the refrigerator (all of five feet away) for something to drink. Seconds later, the plate and fork were exactly as I'd

left them, but there was no sign of the cake — and no telltale crumbs on anyone's snout. So I waited until the next day to investigate just who had done it and how.

Again, I cut off a slice of cake and repeated my movements — and my dog Sam let me in on the mystery of the vanishing cake. He jumped on top of the kitchen table, gingerly approaching the side of the plate where the fork was not, and inhaled the entire slice. Sam was none the worse for his gluttony, thankfully, but many human delicacies can be deadly to animals. Chocolate and alcohol are toxic for all pets; nuts can cause intestinal blockage in ferrets; avocado and rhubarb can kill a bird. The lesson learned: Keep all foodstuffs out of reach of acquisitive paws, whether it's raw liver or a loaf of bread.

As for pet-food storage, bags of dog and cat kibble (not to mention ferret and rabbit feed) should be sealed tightly after they're opened and stored in a container that's impervious to mice and to your pets, who sometimes like to break into their own food supply for between-meal snacks. Covered metal trash cans protect feed bags nicely; they're available at any hardware store. Celebrity animal trainer Bill Berloni prefers Crate & Barrel's good-looking Bullet can, a reproduction of an art deco model. In the case of a multispecies animal house, dogs will inevitably covet cat food because it's higher in protein, so if you keep a kibble-filled self-feeder for your cat, be sure it's placed out of your dog's reach.

Another option is to decant dry kibble into an airtight plastic container, such as the wall-mounted Pour & Store dispenser by Blitz, which holds up to forty pounds of feed. If you've got more than one species of pet, be sure to mark which container holds which species of kibble. Then buy a handy scoop and you're ready to sling hash. Canned food should never be left out all day; if your pets haven't emptied their bowls or plates in twenty minutes, it's time to retrieve the food, cover it with plastic wrap or return it to its can, cover the can with a plastic lid (available at any pet-supply store), and refrigerate for no longer than a day.

Left: Seen and herd: The talented Ms. Lippert and (from left) Arthur, Buddy, and Nocci — three of the four pairs of eyes trained on her whenever she cooks.

When you're done cooking and eating, be sure your garbage and recyclables are stowed in a pet-proof receptacle, preferably out of reach. Otherwise, like Templeton the rat in *Charlotte's Web,* your critters will help themselves to a veritable smorgasbord, having a field day with your trash and tossing it hither and yon. (My dogs particularly love to chomp on stray cat-food tins, as if doing this could somehow bring back the emptied contents.) Then again, some pet people are so creative, they find a way to put even recyclables to tasteful use. Seen Lippert is one of America's most gifted chefs; her innovative cuisine has been savored by Hillary Clinton, Bette Midler, and Jann Wenner. She lives with two Shih tzus, Arthur and Buddy, and two cats with Italian food names, Miel (honey) and Nocci (nuts). Seen developed one of her signature desserts, the Cat Torte, while tinkering about in her kitchen at home. This flourless chocolate delicacy was born because Seen ran out of ring molds and substituted an empty cat-food tin! (Of course, she cleaned it thoroughly first.) "I always have four sets of eyes on me while I cook," she says. Another esteemed chef whose pet keeps her company in the kitchen is the prolific cookbook author Marion Cunningham, who says that her favorite kitchen feature is her golden retriever, Rover. Meanwhile, I was especially proud to be a lifetime fan of the magnetic Patti LaBelle when she made an appearance recently as a guest on *Emeril Live.* The author of *LaBelle Cuisine* stole the show by announcing that she loves garlic "because it smells like my dog, Maximus"!

Incidentally, the expression "I wouldn't feed it to my dog" is starting to be a thing of the past. These days, we're more likely to hear "Nothing's too good for my pet." And nowhere is that enlightened ethic more evident than in the kitchen. Many people are taking the time to prepare meals for their dogs and cats from scratch, whether it's a cooked or raw diet. In December of 1998, Jeffrey Steingarten, *Vogue's* esteemed food critic, devoted several of the magazine's pages to an entertaining exploration of haute homemade options for Sky King, his golden retriever. Jeff included input, insights, and recipes from a few of his friends, including the world-famous chefs Jean-Georges Vongerichten and Daniel Boulud.

Even if they haven't got time to cook, pet lovers are stopping to check the ingredients in their pets' food — just as they do when food shopping for themselves — and opting for brands free of by-products and low in ash. Yet many supermarkets continue to display pet foods in the same aisle as household cleaners that aren't fit for anyone's consumption. This is an outdated attitude, that what we feed our four-legged family members is completely separate from and inferior to what we feed ourselves and our kids. Sadly, in the case of certain pet-food brands, it's true: They're made of meats and grains deemed unfit for human consumption and treated with strong chemical preservatives. Some even carry a warning label discouraging humans from ingesting the contents. Why do you think the cut-rate brands are so inexpensive? Because you get what you pay for.

Fortunately, all that is starting to change as forward-thinking pet-food companies offer health-conscious options on the theory that one is what one eats — and we'd prefer that our beloved pets stay well. These days, Purina looks good enough to eat. Spurning by-products and fillers, Azmira, Canidae and Felidae, Natura Pet (makers of Innova and California Natural), Old Mother Hubbard (maker of Wellness), Pinnacle, Solid Gold, and Wysong are marketing wholesome pet foods with human-grade meats and grains, plus vegetables, fruits, herbs, and antioxidants. And some pet lovers are going so far as to sample their pets' food themselves. At last year's prestigious Gold Medal Food and Beverage Awards ceremony, held at New York's Carnegie Hall, an organic, kosher dog treat called Howlin' Gourmet made culinary history as the first-ever pet food to be honored with an American Tasting Institute (A.T.I.) Award of Excellence (other honorees included Beck's Light and Orville Redenbacher). And yes, chef and A.T.I. national director Jesse Sartain sampled the winning dog treat himself! The treats that

Below left: Esmeralda the cat eats from a Wedgwood cat bowl designed by Nick Munro.

Below right: If you and your guests are enjoying a formal dinner, why not set a place on the floor for your dog? Wedgwood's basalt dog bowl looks splendid on a bone-shaped leather place mat.

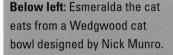

Below: For the cat who has everything, Sylvester's Fiesta cat bowls on a Crate & Barrel place mat make a citrusy-fresh setting.

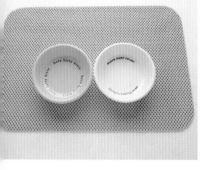

win the blue ribbon in my animal house, however, are Good Buddy Cookies by Castor & Pollux. I couldn't resist the beautiful purple box with its terrific graphic design, and my dogs practically speak English when they catch a whiff of the contents: cheese-, peanut butter–, or carob-flavored biscuits. Believe it or not, I'm pleased to report that I discovered Good Buddy Cookies at my local supermarket. Soon, I'm confident we'll see the day when *all* supermarket pet foods are wholesome enough to be sold alongside the corresponding products for humans, and cans of dog and cat food will be located closer to the baby food than the chemicals.

If you scoff at the very idea of gourmet dog food, you probably think it's going way over the top to serve your pets' meals in ceramic bowls. But pet "tableware" has come a long way since the days of the lightweight plastic double bowl. Consider Wedgwood's jasperware dog and cat bowls, the brainchild of British designer Nick Munro. With their subtle details — a bas-relief bone (for dogs) or fish skeleton (for cats) — these objects are so chic, some petless people might be tempted to acquire them for their good looks alone. Don't laugh. When Sylvester's, a store in the resort town of Sag Harbor, New York, introduced genuine Fiesta bowls for dogs and cats, they were a monster hit. One customer, I'm told, bought two of the dog bowls in cobalt blue to place on her kitchen floor — and she didn't even have a dog. She simply loved the way the bowls looked.

In the decades since its debut in 1936, brightly colored Fiesta ware has become highly collectible, popularized in recent years by people who know from good design (one famous Fiesta collector was the late Andy Warhol). Fiesta is such a fixture on the American scene, it can even be found in the permanent collection of the Smithsonian in Washington, D.C. The West Virginia–based Homer Laughlin China Company discontinued its famous product in 1972 and relaunched it in 1986. As customized for Sylvester's, the dog bowls bear the legend "Good Dog," and the inside of the cat bowls reads "Here Kitty Kitty" or (in homage to Jimi Hendrix) "Move Over Rover Kitty's Taking Over." At under $20 each, they're a highly justifiable luxury.

You think it's shockingly frivolous to spend good money on a ceramic bowl for your pet? Think again. Pets — especially cats — are extremely sensitive to the way things taste, and many would rather forgo drinking altogether than swallow plastic-flavored water. Abstinence from water can lead to more than just dehydration; over the long term, vets point out, it can cause serious kidney trouble. If you must use plastic bowls, be sure to keep them clean and to replace them when they become scratched so bacteria have no chance to multiply. Most important, monitor your pets' drinking habits. If

it looks as though they're not touching their water for long periods of time, switch to metal or ceramic bowls without delay.

Some high-end pet products carry three- and four-figure price tags. London-based pet lover Sheila Parness created a crystal dog bowl engraved with the legend *Fidelis et Constans* (Latin for "Faithful and True") that retails for $395. At the tony Manhattan store Z-Spot, on upper Madison Avenue, an elaborate mosaic dining table, outfitted with two removable stainless-steel bowls, will set you back a mere $1,100. At Z-Spot, four-legged shoppers are too refined to drink what comes out of the tap, despite New York water's worldwide renown. So, like guests at a fancy art opening, they're offered Fiji Natural Artesian water. Incidentally, many pet lovers across the country insist on giving their pets purified water, whether it's filtered on the tap or bottled at the source. Again, it's a case of nothing's too good for our pets.

While expensive products are certainly impressive in cases where money is no object, keep in mind that spending big bucks on pet products doesn't necessarily mean you're getting a lot of design value. As with any other product carrying a steep price tag, let the buyer beware. Besides, from a design standpoint, there's no earthly reason a pet's bowl has to say "Woof" or "Meow." Does your cereal bowl say "Human" or "Yum"? I vote for taking the kitsch out of the animal-house kitchen. Cute is one thing; cutesy is something else. It's entirely possible to buy great design without breaking the bank. K9 Sport makes a terrific-looking injection-molded plastic bowl that's weighted on the inside so it won't travel around on the floor. How good-looking is it? Enough to inspire

Above left: Mr. Brown's people are Victoria and Richard Mackenzie-Childs, Madison Avenue purveyors of artisan pottery, so his feeding arrangement is more elaborate than most: terra-cotta-glazed slipware pastry stands ringed with animal charms, each topped by a coordinating plate and bowl.

Above right: We live in a dog-eat-dog world, so it's only fitting that my B takes her meals at a banquet table custom made in her image by the Santa Fe–based Delilah Enterprises.

Right: Daisy the Norwich terrier drinks only filtered water from a water purifier mounted onto Shannon McLean's faucet.

114

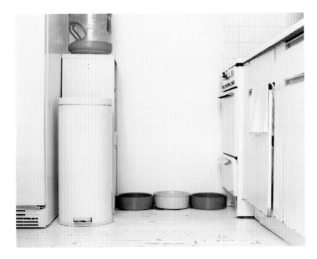

me to coordinate a tableau in my home office with the bowl, a matching place mat and dog bed, and . . . my tangerine iMac!

For my money, some of the best-looking, most functional ceramic bowls around are made by the Robinson Ransbottom Pottery Company of Roseville, Ohio. These plain stoneware beauties are homespun yet elegant, with a simple blue crown decoration. Not only are they notable for not being overdesigned, they're also dishwasher safe. No wonder they're bestsellers at Restoration Hardware. Besides, these bowls have stood up to my crew of hungry dogs for many years now. Even more no-frills are Robinson Ransbottom's Kitty and Dog bowls, which say, simply, "Kitty" or "Dog." Available in one size for cats (5 inches) and three sizes for dogs (5, 7, and 9 inches), they can be mail-ordered directly from Robinson Ransbottom.

Many nondesigner pet bowls are coming up to speed too. If you'd like to upgrade from cheap plastic, but you're not sure about ceramic (or your pets tend to really rough up their bowls at mealtime), opting for metal is the best compromise. Stainless-steel bowls come in matte or high-sheen finishes, and many are trimmed with industrial-cool black rubber nonskid rings to prevent slipping and tipping. They perform as beautifully as they look — and they're lightweight and machine washable to boot.

Many antiques buffs like to designate a vintage bowl or two as their pets' china. Thrift shops and flea markets — especially the legendary outdoor sales at Brimfield, Massachusetts — can be wonderful hunting grounds for such items. I once scored ten incredible Wedgwood saucers, in mint condition, for fifty cents apiece; at another thrift shop, I found some Myott dessert plates. These plates are way too delicate to serve my big dogs with, but they're just right for the cats. In his kitchen, interior designer James Fairfax displays his impressive collection of nineteenth-century lusterware and Staffordshire. Silly, James's cat, has his own Staffordshire tray, plus two coordinated bowls, one for food and the other for water. If you decide to go the vintage route, know that the occasional chipped edge is okay, but be careful to check for deep cracks down the center of the bowl or plate, as they are breeding grounds for bacteria (in this case, really ancient bacteria). In these days of heightened awareness of our pets' well-being,

Above: In Gabriele Sanders's pet-friendly home, even the water is an expression of love: It's none other than Poland Spring.

the idea that a basically unusable piece of china is "good enough" for the dog or cat is passé. If you wouldn't eat from it yourself or feed your kids with it, you shouldn't give it to your pet either.

Whether you opt for stainless steel or Wedgwood bowls, a place mat is a must, especially with big dogs. Not only will it keep the bowls from skidding along on the floor and possibly breaking, it can prevent you and your dog from tripping on them, and it localizes errant splashing, making cleanup much easier. This will help preserve your kitchen floor, especially if, like mine, it's wood. As with pet bowls, most pet-specific place mats tend to be over-the-top cute, complete with illustrations or photographs of animals. Instead, use any one of the cheap and cheerful plastic place mats available at

Left: In Joe Dolce's kitchen, the pet bowls are every bit as high-tech chic as the periwinkle hydraulic stools by Magis.

Crate & Barrel, or check out Target's recycled-rubber mats, designed to resemble cork.

No matter what material it's made of or how decoratively it's adorned, inscribed, or otherwise tarted up, a pet's water bowl simply isn't stylish if it's not kept clean and filled with fresh, clean water. Bowls should be washed regularly, just like your own tableware, to prevent bacteria buildup — especially if your pet eats canned food instead of dry kibble. I read a factoid about the actress Doris Day that endeared her to me forever. Apparently, the founder of the Doris Day Animal League likes to drop in on people who have adopted the league's rescued pets, just to make sure the new home meets with her approval. An important criterion: the levels in the water bowls. So keep those bowls filled, or Doris will be right over. And you wouldn't want her to find them dry, would you?

8.
BATH TIME FOR BONZO

*O*f the many euphemisms offered by dog owners to describe canine elimination, "going to the bathroom" seems like one of the silliest. Pets may poop or do their business — but *go* to the *bathroom?* Absurd. Or is it?

Sara Whalen runs a very special animal sanctuary called Pets Alive in Middletown, New York. I was intrigued when Sara told me about a sweet white dog named Ivory

whose owner was kind enough to bring the dog to Pets Alive the night before he went to jail. Now, Sara is one tough customer who (very wisely) submits all potential adopters to a thorough interview process. In this case, Sara even required something extra: The potential adopter had to have a shower stall, or Ivory could not go home.

This may sound like an odd prerequisite for adoption. But Ivory's owner had trained her to "go" in the shower stall if and when he wasn't able to make it home in time for her walk — which, apparently, was quite often. Ivory had grown accustomed to this routine and, dogs being creatures of habit, Sara didn't want Ivory placed in a situation where she wouldn't be able to do what came naturally. (Incidentally, lucky Ivory was ultimately adopted by a lovely young couple, and yes, their bathroom has a shower stall that Ivory's glad to use as her commode.)

Something about a pet so considerate of her guardian's property really touched me. Since then, I've heard story after story of clever dogs and cats who do, quite liter-

Right: Ann's happy to do her thing in the shower stall — and Todd's happy to encourage her.

Below: Toulouse and Emma, Anna-Sophia Leone's African grays, hang out in the bathroom.

ally, "go to the bathroom." My friend Lori's cat uses the toilet for its intended purpose! Another friend, Stephanie, told me how grateful she was to her dog Victor when, suddenly compelled to heed nature's call, he used the bathtub so as to leave a much more easily cleanable mess for her when she came home from work. Ann, Todd Oldham's Jack Russell terrier, is so intelligent she actually bathroom trained herself. Todd had only to put a Wee-Wee Pad down on the tiled shower-stall floor once

for Ann to understand that that's where she could empty her bladder and bowels if she had to. It's a trick that comes in especially handy if it's the deep of winter, we're feeling — pardon the pun — dog tired, and we haven't got a backyard or terrace to call our own. Even if your home does have a yard, it's a bad idea to leave your dog outside all day, as they become easy prey for neighbors or passersby with cruel intentions. Too many horror stories abound of dogs stolen from their own backyards, or poisoned — so please, don't leave pets outdoors unattended.

Whether or not your dog masters Ann's nifty trick, the bathroom as a whole is an important place in any animal house. When I was growing up, my family's puli used the bathtub not as a water closet but as a safe haven from thunder, lightning, and Fourth-of-July fireworks — all of which sent her running for cover behind the shower curtain, teeth chattering and tail wedged firmly between her legs. A lot of dogs seek shelter in the bathroom; something about that tiled, porcelain-intense room offers comfort like no other place in the home. It tends to be the coolest area in the house (unless, of course, someone's just taken a hot shower), and when animals are stressed, they naturally seek a place to "chill out." Dog trainer Bash Dibra, who's brought to heel the pets of Sarah Jessica Parker, Mariah Carey, and Henry Kissinger, compares the "paw-celain" nesting instinct to wolves' digging in the ground, where they feel cool and safe.

Then there are the instances when animals seek out the bathroom *because* it's hot and humid. Anna-Sophia Leone's parrots love keeping her company in the shower. They were bred in captivity, but you can't take the jungle out of the bird, and a steamy bathroom is a kind of man-made rainforest that simulates the climate conditions in these creatures' natural habitat. Anna-Sophia's African grays especially treasure their bathroom time, using her chrome-plate towel bar as a combination perch–jungle gym.

No corner of a bathroom goes unused in an animal house. In any other species of home, etiquette dictates that the toilet seat cover always be returned to the down posi-

Below left: All dogs would if they could. Daisy just happens to be too short!

Below right: Weegee, Anne Fisher's bearded collie, only drinks from the toilet bowl. If that is your dog's beverage preference, be sure to keep the toilet clear of automatic bowl cleaners. When cleaning the bowl, use a gentle scouring agent like Bon Ami and flush repeatedly until no more suds are visible.

Right: Max curled up in the sink.

Below: Lucky Blaze — her human, firefighter Timmy Haskell, bathes her himself instead of sending her to the groomer.

tion. According to the principles of feng shui, one should put the lid down to prevent the inauspicious outflow of wealth. But in an animal house, the lid generally stays up, for the toilet often winds up being a favorite watering hole for those breeds of dog tall enough to get their snouts in the bowl. Actually, animal-welfare groups such as People for the Ethical Treatment of Animals (PETA) advocate leaving the seat up so if Fido's water bowl runs dry while you're away, or some kind of emergency keeps you from home, the toilet can provide a clean supply of the vital wet stuff that could prove a lifesaver. Obviously, if your dogs drink from the toilet, refrain from using automatic bowl cleaners. Also, stay away from newfangled water closets that come with built-in disinfectants and deodorizers, which are also toxic if swallowed. No pets should ever drink a chemical quaff!

The sink, meanwhile, doubles as a lovely perch for a cat in search of a relaxing place to meditate. The sight of Kitty curled up in the basin is a familiar one to many of us with cats. Just be sure the basin is stable enough to support your cat's weight. And try to keep the sinkside area clear of soap, toothpaste, shaving lotion, and all manner of gunk — you wouldn't want your cats licking it off themselves or the sink. Remember to wipe the basin dry after you're done using it so Kitty doesn't get herself uncomfortably wet or track dampness all over your home. On the other

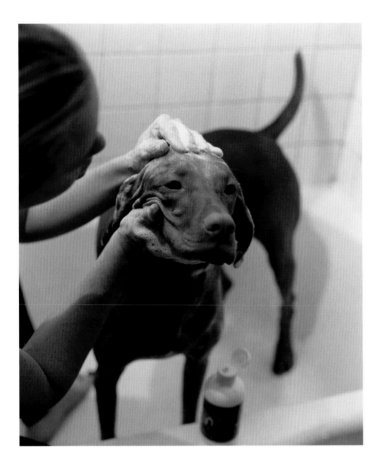

hand, a slightly leaky cold tap can be a heaven-sent source of hydration to a feline who prefers her water supply clean, cool, and fresh. The sink is also a fine place to wash your small pet. Bigger dogs, however, obviously require the bathtub if you haven't got a yard to hose them down in.

My white dog, Daisy, is the soul of elegance: She's shopped at Hermès and Bergdorf Goodman, had her portrait drawn by Robert Risko for *The New Yorker,* been stroked by Naomi Campbell and smiled at by (at different times) Helen Mirren and Mia Farrow as they passed her on the street. Still, if I don't keep a close watch on Daisy in the park, I'll discover too late that she's done that atavistic doggy thing and rubbed her face and neck in some other creature's poop, necessitating something she scarcely bargained for: a bath.

Coming clean is a sensitive issue in petland. Sending dogs to a professional groomer is advisable in the case of pets who grow distressed at the mere suggestion of that four-letter *B* word, as a frantic dog can seriously injure himself struggling on the lavatory's slippery surfaces. So if your pet hates being bathed, locate a reputable groomer in your neighborhood and leave the sudsing to them.

But then, animals can get stressed at the groomer's too. In major cities, where no expense is spared for the comfort of our pets, certain groomers will make house calls so that animals can be beautified in the comfort of their own home. The cost? On average $100 per hour, provided you can secure an appointment. These services are more coveted than last-minute bookings with hairdresser Frédéric Fekkai. One dog groomer

who specializes in house calls begged me not to name him; his services were already so much in demand that he didn't want to be put in the unpopular position of having to turn people away.

If you undertake to bathe your pets yourself, remember to avoid human shampoos. Their pH level is not dog friendly, and regular use of adult human shampoo on canine skin can lead to an itchy pet in need of veterinary attention. There are plenty of stylish shampoo options for pets, including Origins Silky Coat dog shampoo, Espree Beauty Without Cruelty hypoallergenic shampoo, and Earthbath, which comes in a range of scrumptious scents, including Mango Tango. I predict that in the near future, we'll be able to one-stop-shop at beauty stores like Sephora for species-specific shampoos for ourselves *and* our pets. Already there's a designer fragrance called Oh My Dog!, created for people and their dogs to share — and believe it or not, it smells lovely! Aesop recently introduced Animal, a gentle shampoo made with lemon rind, tea tree oil, and peppermint leaf that humans can share with their cats and dogs, and Fauna offers an entire range of trans-species beauty products, including sunscreen. If these products aren't available near you, use the mildest baby shampoo you can find.

Bath time can be an opportunity for quality togetherness. Although cats are perfectly capable of grooming themselves (with the exception of Persians, Himalayans, and other long-haired breeds, who require daily brushing to keep their coats healthy and mat free), some of them enjoy keeping us company while we're soaking in the tub. Maximize this shared time by, say, bringing a teaser into the bath with you and exercising Kitty with it while you soak. You can relax in the tub while Kitty does aerobics on the bathroom floor.

For obvious reasons, the cat litter box is most often located in the bathroom: It is a kitty toilet, after all (ferrets and rabbits use litter boxes too). In homes with cats, the litter box is frequently the first thing one sees upon entering the bathroom — and let's face it, a litter box is not the most attractive object in the world.

Nowadays, when high-end product designers are spiffing up every imaginable object from toilet brushes to robe hooks, it's a mystery to me why some savvy American manufacturer hasn't yet devised a good-looking litter box. It's especially perplexing considering that litter boxes must be made of plastic (cat urine is too corrosive to be contained by anything else), a favorite working material of designers such as Philippe Starck and Karim Rashid. We connect the world via the Internet, shuttle people into deep space . . . but we can't make a good-looking litter box? Whoever finally does create a stylish model is certain to be a hero to design-conscious cat lovers everywhere. And take it from me, cat lovers are some of the *most* design-conscious people out there. In the meantime, one option is the Cateau, brainchild of San Francisco–based architect Brier Tomlinson. It's a decorative corrugated cardboard box that fits around a litter box and cheers it up enormously.

Still, many people don't even think about how a litter box looks; they're too offended by the way it smells. Cat litter is one of the most absorbent substances around — one of the prime ingredients of litter recently proved useful in the cleanup of radioactive waste! Even so, cat litter needs your help to do its job well. No matter what kind you use, whether traditional (clay), high-tech (silica gel formed into little white desiccant pearls) or all-natural (products made of corn, wheat, or pine), please don't try to prolong its shelf life. Change the litter at the first nose-wrinkling whiff of ammonia. That usually means a complete litter overhaul once a week without fail (unless you happen to be using my personal favorite brand, World's Best Cat Litter, which is made of clumping, odor-beating, whole-kernel corn and lasts as long as thirty days with one cat and fifteen days with two). Placing a rubber mat in front of the box helps cut down on litter being tracked through the house.

And please, rake and scoop the litter at least once a day, for your own sake as well as your cat's. It's a form of furniture protection: A cat who deems his litter box unusable is

Left: Layla the kitten supervises the litter-box cleanup. Lining the pan with garbage bags can help ease the chore of overhauling the litter. If your cat tends to give the box a hearty scratch after each use, avoid messy accidents by being prepared with an extra bag — just in case Kitty's nails have turned the liner into a sieve.

very likely to select a place that will really get your attention — such as the middle of your bed — to make his protest as clear as possible. And who can blame Kitty? How would you feel if you had to stand ankle-deep in a toilet nobody ever cleaned and you were powerless to clean it yourself? That is every domestic cat's plight. And most of them would, understandably, rather go elsewhere in the house than muck about in a dirty box. If your cat relieves himself in an inappropriate place, don't resent him: He's simply alerting you to a problem, and it's up to you to solve it. If you were in his boots, you'd probably stage a similar protest, and you'd be justified. Sadly, too many cats wind up abandoned in shelters because they didn't use their litter box. But nobody bothers to mention that's probably because their people didn't keep those litter boxes clean. So keep that litter clean no matter how the box looks, because a clean cat box is always stylish.

It sounds obvious, but don't forget to leave the door to the bathroom open. In most polite homes, we're taught to close the bathroom door behind us. But in an animal house, if the litter's in the bathroom, the door must stay at least partially open so Kitty has unlimited access to her box. If you prefer to keep it closed, create an opening at the bottom of the door that's big enough for Kitty to pass through. (The ever-elegant French call this a *chatière*.)

People for whom aesthetics are a priority are bound to devise ingenious solutions to the litter-box problem, even if it means moving kitty's loo out of the bathroom and into a closet rigged with a kitty door. At James Blauvelt's stately Hamptons home, the litter box used by his cat, Bundle, is artfully concealed beneath a cluster of spathiphyllum plants in one corner of the elegant dining room. Interior designer James Fairfax carved a perfect little archway into the kitchen cabinet that hides the under-sink area in his kitchen; now it also hides his litter box — and Silly the cat quickly learned where to go. An additional advantage to these types of arrangements: The cats in question get a lot more privacy in which to do their business. And extra privacy is always a treat, in an animal house or any other species of home.

Speaking of loos, have you ever come home to a floor strewn with shredded bathroom tissue? Thinking it was the paper's scent that compelled my cats to use it as a

scratching surface, I tried every unscented brand on the market, even spending extra on recycled "green" toilet paper from the health-food store. The effect was the same: Certain cats, namely my gray male, Pushkin, simply *had* to shred the toilet paper, gleefully unrolling it all over the bathroom like ticker tape at a parade. Finally, a lightbulb went on: I bought and installed a hooded metal toilet-paper roller. The hood prevented Pushkin from getting at the toilet paper — and put an end to my months of frustration. Okay, so it's a bit institutional. But it cuts down on cleanup and keeps me from being annoyed with my cat.

For safety's sake, avoid glass containers in the bathroom. Nothing cuts our animals' paw pads quite as cruelly as broken glass, which has a way of shattering into a million microscopic switchblades when it collides with the tub or sink. Stick with beauty products in unbreakable plastic packages. If you like to display flowers in the bathroom, use plastic vessels such as By Bing's flexible one or Harry Gutfreund's Plastic Fantastic, both available at the Museum of Modern Art Design Store, or consider Pottery Barn's clear plastic shower curtain with pockets big enough for small blooms. A first-aid kit is a must for the animal-house bathroom. It should include items such as antibiotic ointment (for cuts), Nolvasan (a bactericidal rinse), and bandages to wrap injured paws with. As for what to use to spot-clean every bathroom surface from the toilet to the litter box, I keep a big plastic jug of plain white vinegar in there. It's a brilliant degreaser and antiseptic, it's nontoxic if licked, and combined with baking soda and a mild dish-washing detergent, it foams up to make an excellent scrubbing agent.

Left: Three spathiphyllum plants in James Blauvelt's dining room do more than add lush greenery to the space; they conceal the litter box used by his cat, Bundle.

Below: Fresh flowers improve the atmosphere anywhere. In an animal house they should be arranged in something unbreakable, like Harry Gutfreund's adorable plastic vases.

9.
UP TO SNIFF

*W*hen you live with pets, invisible atmospherics are as crucial as visible furnishings. They range from the way your animal house smells to the way it sounds to the humidity level.

Our shared spaces should be as easy on the nostrils as they are on the eyes. Dust bunnies are not the sort of pet anyone wants! It's crucial to keep a clean home, as letting filth pile up in an animal house is tantamount to animal cruelty. And believe me, filth does have a way of piling up. That said, in my interviews with dozens of pet lovers, I

keep hearing the following refrain: "I clean up less after the dog/cat than I do after my kids/husband/boyfriend/girlfriend/you-fill-in-the-blank." One of my prized possessions is a white Florence Knoll table. Wouldn't you know that somebody put a pile of receipts down on that table, then proceeded to spill something liquid over the lot. The purple ink from one of those tiny documents is permanently printed on that beautiful white tabletop, despite my best efforts to remove it, so I'll always be reminded of how much was spent on groceries that day. Our pets don't create nearly as much mess as we do — they're just easy targets for blame.

Still, there will be times when your pets will track in dirt or produce foul odors, so you need to stay alert. What if the neighbors caught a whiff of an animal house that hadn't been cleaned in a week — on a rainy day, which makes odors even more pungent, or on a day when one of the animals decided to dispense with housebreaking skills? The neighbors might complain to the landlord about the odor. And what might ensue would not only ruin your day, and possibly your entire year, it would reflect poorly on all animal lovers trying to keep house. As pet lovers, we're a breed apart, and we have to be goodwill ambassadors for our species. Falling off the clean wagon spoils things for all of us, pets and humans alike.

As anyone who's ever cleaned up after pets knows, they leave behind a lot of fluff. But pet lovers have noticed an intriguing phenomenon: If managed properly, pet hair can actually speed the dust-elimination process. Dust bunnies are magnetically attracted to shed hair, forming what architect Robin Elmslie Osler poetically calls "tumbleweeds" that are easily swept up and tossed in the trash. For a really clean sweep, a powerful vacuum cleaner is a must. So many of the people interviewed for this book own Miele vacuum cleaners that it became a running joke that this project was turning into an advertisement for that excellent company. The Miele is a serious machine and a wise investment. Of course, it doesn't come cheap — especially if you get one with a HEPA (High Efficiency Particulate Air) filter, which holds back 99.97 percent of particles sucked in — but it eats such prodigious amounts of detritus that I can't begin to imagine life in my animal house without it.

Whether or not you join the Miele cult, discuss your needs with a vacuum dealer and he'll point you in the right direction. The best part about a vacuum with a HEPA filter? If anyone in your home is allergic to a pet, it helps enable a compromise by cutting down on irritation. "People have told us the machine has let them keep their husbands and cats at the same time," says a Miele spokesman. I don't know about you, but that kind of testimonial gets me to pay more for a high-ticket appliance any day.

Many animal lovers vacuum and dust more than once a week; some do it every day. But if all this talk of cleanup has you cross-eyed, or you're simply too busy or too disinclined to do it yourself, you'll have to seek help. They say good help is hard to find, but it's even tougher locating someone who doesn't mind cleaning up after pets. Be sure to find a housekeeper who isn't allergic to animals, either physiologically or philosophically. Since a good part of the mess in your animal house is sure to be pet related, whether it's urine stains or piles of hair, your housekeeper must be willing to take it all in stride.

I got lucky with my housekeeper. Not only is Theresa an animal lover, she has a Persian cat of her own, so pet-hair-studded dust bunnies are no match for her — plus, she takes breaks in her routine to tease Cyrus, my Persian, with her Dust Caesar, which he's happy to swat at. Theresa is also careful not to open the window without first putting a

Right: Diligent paw cleaning can help prevent mud, salt, and other unsavory substances from being tracked all over your animal house. It also helps keep your dog's pads dry, so moisture won't accumulate between the toes, where it could cause skin problems.

screen in the frame, and to be on the lookout for curious kitties and dogs seeking to escape out the front door or stick their noses where they shouldn't (i.e., in a pail full of mopping suds). Stephen Miller Siegel really hit the jackpot: His housekeeper, Ceta, not only cleans up after his two golden retrievers, she bathes them, walks them, and sings to them. "Our housekeeper, Ana, is our bird's *officina*," says Sheri Holman. "She also loves the cats. They run straight to her, and she loves playing with them." A bird-watching housekeeper is a godsend, as bird cages that aren't cleaned regularly and thoroughly can result in the residents' coming down with skin diseases and mites.

Cut down on the filth quotient by doing a paw check each time you come in from the great outdoors. "The number one thing about having a dog and working with your interior is keeping your dog clean," says Matthew Morris. "That doesn't mean bathing him every week, it just means wiping him down if it's raining or snowing, before he comes back in. I always keep towels and a bottle of water by the door so I can wipe off his paws." That's an especially wise move in winter, when salt scattered on streets and driveways not only irritates dogs' paws, it gets tracked indoors, leaving nasty white deposits. Treat your dog's paw pads with Musher's Secret wax before going out in the cold and keep a little plastic bowl and some water by the front door so that you're prepared to dunk grimy paws in it and wipe them clean before they come inside.

If you're in the country or the park and it's muddy out, by all means dip those paws in warm water and wipe them clean and dry. If you're in an urban setting and it's sweltering outside, be sure to check for melted chewing gum; mineral oil removes it nicely. In general, city dwellers must keep their eyes peeled for anything harmful — or just plain gross — their dogs might be stepping in, including salt (in winter), broken glass, antifreeze (it's bright green and highly toxic if ingested or licked off the paws), rusty nails, and rat poison.

You will also want to take stock of the cleaning products used in your home. Sadly, many detergent megabrands are chemical brews that are quite toxic to people, pets, and the environment. (Worse, they tend to be tested on animals in ways too horrible to get into here; contact People for the Ethical Treatment of Animals for a complete list of green household-cleaning products.) Be aware in choosing cleaning products that many fabric-freshening sprays and other heavily scented products can be harmful to birds. And never, ever spray any household cleaner directly on your pet or his bedding. The Swiffer, on the other hand, is a great idea for bird households — or any animal house, for that matter — because it eliminates the need for spraying; the polish is already on the cloth.

Animal lovers are especially wary of chemicals — not just because they'd rather not expose their best friends to harsh substances, but because they tend to be quite sensitive to the animal-testing issue. It's a safe bet that the majority of people spending extra on everything "green," from detergents to mattresses, are animal lovers.

All told, many animal houses endorse all-natural cleaning products that are never tested on animals, such as Ecover and Seventh Generation. My favorite green product is an all-purpose spray cleaner called Sun and Earth. It's made from a trio of simple, all-natural ingredients — orange oil, coconut oil, and water — and in informal studies conducted in my home, it's outperformed its competitors every time (Sun and Earth also makes laundry and liquid dish-washing detergents). It's especially good for wood floors — the oils condition the floorboards and give them a nice luster. And since pets' tongues frequently make contact with the floor, whether they're chewing bones, licking paws, or nibbling runaway kibble, it's reassuring to know they're not licking up toxic substances. Plus, after I've used Sun and Earth, my whole place smells thoroughly inviting, as if I've been spraying $100-per-ounce designer room fragrance. For a different take on citrus cleaning power, a product called Citrus Magic Air Fragrance combines the pleasantly tart oils of orange, lemon, lime, tangerine, and grapefruit.

The Caldrea Home Care Collection is a line of attractively packaged aromatherapeutic housecleaning products in three different formulas (including Relaxing Lavender-Pine) that look and smell more like designer beauty products. Caldrea is both child- and pet-safe because its inventor, the Minnesota-based Monica Nassif, has two small daughters

Below: Green cleaners earn the animal-house seal of approval.

Below: A fragrant survival kit can dramatically improve an animal house's atmosphere.

and two cats, Prancer and Clara, and wanted to make housecleaning a more positive experience for herself and her loved ones.

If animal-house residents speak of performance cleaning products with quasi-religious fervor, recommending them to one another as we would a beloved veterinarian, it's because they can affect quality of life in no small way. Eleanor Mondale's favorite cleaning product is Nature's Miracle. "We buy it en masse, by the case," she raves, "and we use it everywhere: in the house, in the horse trailer . . . It doesn't smell like anything — it just takes away the odors that you don't want." The makers of a nontoxic, biodegradable all-purpose cleaner called Simple Green even include a testimonial from a dog lover — plus a photo of her dog — in their print advertisements.

Keeping the air smelling lovely is as important as maintaining spotless surfaces. Perfume is no substitute for cleaning, so I'm not suggesting that you mask unpleasant odors but that you keep your place clean first, then populate it with pleasant aromas. (And always take care if you have birds not to spray any perfume near them because of their sensitive respiratory systems.) What with the proliferation of room perfumes on the market, it's no surprise that animal houses are major consumers of environmental fragrances. Some pet-supply stores carry an impressive range of scented candles alongside their selection of foods, litters, and treats (of course, common sense dictates that we never leave a burning wick unattended in an animal house). As it turns out, one of the best fragrances to combat pet odor is also the key ingredient in Sun and Earth: citrus. L'Occitane en Provence makes lovely orange-scented candles, including the delightful clementine; for the winter months, when a richer, heavier fragrance is in order, there's L'Occitane orange-nutmeg and cinnamon-orange. Yet another candle brand that's quite popular with the pet set is Votivo No. 96C, which emits a powerfully delicious red-currant scent. The best part about candles is that, like fashion, you can change them with the seasons. At Christmastime, why not try burning a myrrh candle by Diptyque in honor of the three wise men?

Many pet people have discovered that dried-lavender sachets and natural lavender oil not only smell wonderful, they double as flea repellents. After my "wag room" gets its weekly scrub-down, I apply lavender oil directly to dog beds, floors, baseboards, and the wood parts of the furniture. Aveda sells lavender essential oil (they also have a lavender candle, Lavandou Plant Pure-Fume, that's quite efficient at masking odors). Lavender essential oil can be obtained at your local health-food store too. Just be sure to check that you're really getting essence of lavender, not a lavender scent chemically re-created in a lab, or you won't get the flea-repellent benefit. For those between-bath

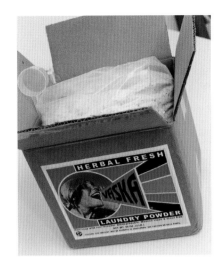

times when a hit of lavender is in order, Earthbath makes lavender Deodorizing Spritz with oatmeal, aloe, and vitamin E to condition your dog's skin and coat. Another of my favorite products is Vaska Herbal Fresh laundry powder, which combines natural soap powder and real dried lavender. The dozens of pounds of laundry my animal house produces weekly used to horrify me. As a die-hard laundry hater, I never thought that washing load after load of dirty clothes could be a delightful experience. But this extraordinary soap manages to bring aromatherapy to a chore that sorely needs it and actually makes doing the wash a pleasure. Plus, it's free of optical brighteners and safe enough to double as a hand soap in a pinch.

While grocery shopping, I came across bottled rose water in the ethnic food aisle (it's used in Lebanese cooking). Although it's quite inexpensive, this stuff has an exquisite aroma to rival the swankest designer fragrances. I've found that a few drops on a guest towel in the bathroom where I keep my litter boxes has the power to improve the atmosphere in there immediately (the cats seem to like it too).

Wonderful as natural lavender is, fragrances produced in test tubes have their own special advantages. One of the leaders in man-made fragrance technology is Demeter Fragrance Library, which makes offbeat signature scents like Sushi, Ginger Ale, Grass, Cucumber, Popcorn, Dirt, and Dust, to name just a few. Demeter's Tomato Pick-Me-Up Cologne Spray is a brilliant way to combat pet odors — it neutralizes them faster than a *Star Trek* phaser. "The enzymes in tomato destroy odor-causing bacteria," explains Demeter nose Christopher Brosius. "That's the reason tomato has always been recommended to remove the smell of skunk from dogs and people." I've taken to buying the stuff in quantity and spritzing it all over myself and everything I own, including

Above left: For some reason, my little Destiny has more pungent body odor than her pack-mates, and drier skin to boot. The answer to our dilemma: a daily hit of Between Bath Deodorizing Spritz, which comes complete with coat conditioners.

Above center: Lavender is a heaven scent that also repels fleas. I like to use it as often as possible — especially when doing the laundry.

Above right: One excellent way to keep things smelling nice is to put some pet-safe fragrance on your hands and rub down your dog. That's the idea behind Oh My Dog! perfume, which was designed to reinforce the animal-human bond through aromatic message.

the lampshades, the cat carrier, and the car. Walking into Christopher's home, even on a rainy day, the first thing one notices is how good it smells: *really* good. His secret? Several spritzes of tomato spray added to the mopping-up water, and Demeter tomato oil burning in little censers placed at key points around his home. Caswell-Massey makes an inexpensive terra-cotta lamp with a candle beneath and a glazed bowl on top to hold scented oil for an aromatic slow burn. (However and wherever you apply room perfume, be careful never to spray any alcohol-based perfume directly on your pets, as their skin could become irritated.) Recently, Demeter introduced an environmental fragrance technology that's nothing short of revolutionary: a water-based fragrance called Unscented designed with a special complex that adheres to curtains, sheets, and upholstery fabrics, and eats lingering odors right out of them.

Chatting with Christopher, I wondered why he hadn't introduced a scent in honor of his mastiff, a gentle giant named Zephyr. Well, Christopher was way ahead of me: He was already in the final stages of capturing and bottling three scents we animal lovers know all too well: Paws, Wet Dog, and Puppy. By the way, some of us happen to think *eau de chien mouillé* — that's French for essence of wet dog — is one of the most comforting smells in the world. But though essence of clean wet dog is a shiny, happy smell, dirty wet dog is a different story entirely. Be sure to bathe your dogs as often as your vet says is healthy, especially if they have a tendency toward oily skin, which will leave spots and foul odors on your upholstery. Dr. Rebecca Campbell, a vet in private practice in Manhattan, recommends bathing no more than every other week, or you risk drying out your pet's skin.

Humidity is another atmospheric flourish that benefits all residents of an animal house. If you have birds, it's advisable to invest in an air purifier as well. Anna-Sophia Leone has two Vornado VAQS25s with HEPA filters running at all times in her living room for the benefit of her winged pets' sensitive respiratory systems, plus a Bionaire humidifier on either side of their cage during the dry winter months. She also has a humidity meter so she can conveniently keep indoor conditions at a bird-friendly 35 to 45 percent. If you haven't got time for humidifier upkeep, try the low-tech alternative: a pot of water on the radiator. It goes a long way toward making pets — and people — comfortable during a long, dry winter. It can certainly make all the difference to an itchy cat, as it will help keep his skin from drying out and him from overlicking himself, which will in turn cut down on hairballs. Plus, it helps reduce static in the wintertime, when a fingertip brushing past the cat can spark a shock that sends him running.

There are many other creative ways to improve the atmosphere in your animal house.

Opposite: Pictures at an exhibition: Captain Andy and Danny Mann, two of Christine Butler's Cornish Rex cats, look like gallery visitors against the "relationship" wall that helps keep them all in the pink.

Feng shui is the ancient science of decorating a home to improve the residents' health and fortune, and it's become enormously popular in recent years, with book after book on the subject coming out, and feng shui masters such as David Raney (the man who configured Donna Karan's Madison Avenue store) achieving pop-star status.

Photographer Christine A. Butler swears that her life improved dramatically after *Feng Shui Revealed* author R. D. Chin prescribed specific colors of paint for key surfaces in her home. Pittsburgh Paints' Paris Pink was rolled onto her south-facing "relationship" wall to help keep Christine's love life "in the pink." Those good vibes, R. D. told me, logically extend to Christine's four-legged loves, a quartet of Cornish Rex cats named Captain Andy, Danny Mann, Lisette, and Curly Sue.

Feng shui and felines are natural together. R. D. Chin lives with two cats, Boris and Goliath, as well as a miniature schnauzer named Mozart. David Raney created a "kitty altar" for his two cats, Bodhi and Squirrel. "Pets add life to a space," R. D. says. Proving the truth of that statement is the light-filled bedroom of Jean-Claude Huon's beautiful duplex apartment, where a carved Buddha prescribed by *his* feng shui master commands the hearth. Completing this lively picture is a spectacularly minimal arrangement created by New York's l'Olivier. The square of grass framed in fresh bamboo stalks is the favorite stomping ground of Jean-Claude's cat, Zulla.

Arrangements that incorporate grass are quite popular with the fashionable set. In an animal house, grass is not only fresh looking and chic, it serves a wonderful purpose. Cats love grass: Nibbling at it aids their digestion, supplies essential nutrients, and keeps their coats healthy. Plus, they enjoy lying down and napping in a small field of green — especially if they're city cats who aren't (and shouldn't be) permitted to leave their apartments. An arrangement of grass brings the outdoors in, and it's quite simple and inexpensive to grow yourself. "It's become very popular to grow something that's catered toward your cat," explains Nina Humphrey, cat lover and plant buyer at Chelsea Garden Center in New York City. "Grass is cheap, easy, and fun, and it brings a sense of spring into your home. And your cat will love you for it!" Nina recommends laying out flats of wheat grass or oat grass, or cutting them up and planting them in decorative little pots.

Music is an underrated atmosphere enhancer in an animal house. The seventeenth-century playwright William Congreve penned one of the most misquoted lines in the history of literature: "Music has charms to soothe a savage breast." Over the centuries, people substituted "savage beast" so often that the phrase stuck. Music can certainly quiet a savage *beast,* and it also does wonders for domesticated animals. The story of Bumper and Drew and their training crate is a fine example.

Above: When fresh peonies are out of season, Banana Republic's peony fragrance (available in bath oil and room spray) gives an animal house an instant atmospheric lift.

The training crate is an object of no small controversy in petland. There are people who are convinced that it's cruel to keep a dog in a cage, but reputable dog trainers everywhere insist that the crate is a positive thing, providing Fido with a little room, or den, that's all his own. A crate can be a valuable tool to help you train a pup not to pee or poop indoors — and a well-trained dog is more likely not to wind up at a shelter "because he went in the house." Being dumped at a shelter is obviously the much more cruel fate, and it's completely avoidable if we use crates humanely. When the crate becomes cruel is when people confine dogs to a crate for long hours (that's like making a large person sit in an economy airline seat all day, every day) or when they keep the crate off to the side, away from the action, resulting in a lonely, stressed-out dog.

Unfortunately, the majority of crate manufacturers don't take aesthetics into account, and crates wind up looking the way the anticrate camp perceives them: like mini-prisons. And so they wind up being positioned somewhere in the house that's "out of sight, out of mind." I wish an inspired architect would redesign the crate so it actually looked sculptural and decorative. Then fewer pets would miss out on the action while doing crate time. In the best taking-lemons-and-making-lemonade tradition, imaginative people manage to make do beautifully with the available crate selection. While

training their two puppies, Bumper and Drew, Joe Dolce and Jonathan Burnham set up the most stylish crate arrangement imaginable. They positioned the girls' Midwest crate beside the Steinway baby grand, so that Jonathan could play soothing jazz standards for them as they drifted off to sleep. (And the black epoxy coating on the crate coordinates nicely with the glossy black finish on the piano.)

For those pets who don't share digs with a piano man, recorded music is a fine way to unwind. Tape your own soothing pet tunes, or check out *Pet Music,* an ASPCA-endorsed, three-CD set of mellow instrumentals designed to reduce pets' stress. Chitra Besbroda operates a no-kill shelter in New York City called Sentient Creatures. Each evening at bedtime, her adoptable charges listen to lullabies by Brahms! If you have to leave town and your dog has the pleasure of staying at Rondout Valley Kennels in Accord, New York, the boarding facility offers kennels where classical melodies are piped in for your pet's listening pleasure. And all that is music to our ears.

Now that you've put all this effort into creating a stylish, clean, fragrant, harmonious home, you'll want to show it off to your friends. Before you go about creating party atmosphere, bone up on training basics with your dog by practicing key commands such as "Sit" and "Stay" — these will enable you to discourage him from overwhelming guests at the door and scarfing your carefully presented canapés. You could also teach your party animal a special trick, such as greeting the guests by sitting and letting them pet him hello. Linda Lambert's mutt, Trusty, taught himself a special party trick. Linda entertains often in her splendid dining room, decorated in the Regency Brighton Pavilion style with a mahogany table and red lacquer rattan chairs. When one of Linda's guests rises to visit the loo, Trusty calmly jumps up and keeps that person's seat warm, politely refraining from touching the table or the plates on it. Visitors don't seem to mind; the only one in recent memory who did "never came back," Linda reports. (Good riddance!)

When party planning, compile your guest list with care. Make sure the people you invite aren't allergic to animals and debrief them on party pet-iquette: Request that they refrain from smoking (especially if you have birds) and feeding your pets toxic treats such as chocolate or alcohol. Give skittish cats their own room behind a closed door so they don't get frightened by what they perceive as hordes of giants swarming their space; you don't want Kitty running out into the hallway and possibly the street. Keep a close eye on ferrets whenever liquor is flowing, as they have a thing for beer and wine, and will lap at spills that aren't healthy for them. As for birds, sequester them too, so that they won't be overwhelmed by party-hearty revelers trying to slip them contraband edibles. Just in case, make sure all pets have on collars with ID tags, so that if someone does slip out he has a chance of being found. With a little extra planning and attention to detail, everyone in your animal house can survive a party healthy, happy, and stress free — including you.

Atmosphere is never more important than during the holidays, but certain holiday decorations can be quite harmful to pets. Contrary to what you may have heard, poinsettia is not deadly to furred friends (though it is toxic) — but, warns animal nutritionist Rosaly Grunberg of New York's Canine Concepts, several other yuletide flora are, namely mistletoe, ivy, holly berries, eucalyptus, fir trees, Chinese evergreen, and a plant called Christmas rose.

When setting up your Christmas tree, place it in a room where you can limit your pets' access to it, and anchor it securely to the wall; active animals have been known to bring trees crashing down on themselves accidentally. Always wrap the tree snugly with a towel or blanket so

Below: Please pass the jelly: Trusty the mutt always makes sure seats vacated by Linda Lambert's guests stay warm — and he never steals from their plates.

curious pets can't drink the water the trunk is standing in (which may contain toxic fertilizers). Forgo lights (pets can chew the wires and electrocute themselves), glass balls (pets mistake them for toys, but if chewed and swallowed the razor-sharp shards can kill), the tiny wire hangers commonly used to attach ornaments to the tree (pets can choke on them, so use ribbons instead), and tinsel and icicles (if swallowed, the festive strands can cause serious, and sometimes fatal, damage to a pet's intestines).

Despite all these restrictions, it *is* possible to decorate a beautiful tree that won't harm your pets. Instead of glass, opt for ornaments made of wood, fabric, cardboard, and paper. Feeling crafty? Try your hand at origami, and fold white, gold, or silver paper into cranes, then thread string through the top and hang. Or laminate photographs or drawings of your pets and tie them to the tree branches with red or white grosgrain ribbon. Sheer gold polyester ribbon is so elegant you won't even miss the tinsel and icicles; thread the ribbon in a spiral around the tree or tie bows directly to the branch tips.

Fresh flowers make great tree ornaments. Carnations smell wonderful and stay fresh longer than any other cut flower — plus, in white or red, they look dynamite against dark green branches. Keeping them fresh is simple: Attach water-filled plastic vials from your florist. As for what goes under the pet-safe tree, that's up to you. Just don't leave unwrapped presents lying about and toss out gift wrap at once, so curious pets won't have a chance to devour the ribbon, which can also cause intestinal damage. And never, ever give a puppy, kitten, or any other species of creature as a gift, because animals are not commodities. What if the person couldn't keep the pet and the animal wound up euthanized at a shelter? Buy and wrap a stuffed animal instead.

Left: All spruced up: the pet-safe tree in the lobby of the Humane Society of New York. Merry Christmas!

10.
PAWS FOR SAFETY

W hat, exactly, is a stylish home for pets? A safe habitat that feels as good as it looks, for the four-legged residents as well as the two-legged ones. Whatever choices you make in your decor, safety should always be top of mind in an animal house. And the key to a safe habitat is pet-proofing your home.

We childproof our homes; why not apply those same safety measures to a home with pets? As with childproofing, pet-proofing works two ways: It involves making a home safe for pets *and* protecting our belongings *from* pet damage. Balancing the two — pet safety and furniture preservation — is a high-wire act responsible animal-house-keepers perform daily.

Pet-proofing starts with a sticker on the front door conveying a message along the lines of, "In Case of Emergency, Please Save Our Pets," with space for you to fill in the number and type of pets police officers or firefighters will find inside. The trouble is, these stickers tend to be eyesores. As a result, many people are disinclined to mar the front door with them (plus, they're quite difficult to remove when no longer needed). But, as I hope we've proved, there's no reason style and function can't cohabit peacefully in an animal house. After I wondered aloud why some inspired animal-loving graphics whiz never came up with a better solution, to the rescue came Tim Convery, who created a safety sticker that's the perfect marriage of beauty and utility. I'd like to see it produced as both a magnet (for the front door) and an easy-to-remove static-film decal (for the windows). The story of the emergency sticker is a good reminder that design is important: It helps us keep products we need

Right: Tim Convery's emergency sticker can be customized according to the number and type(s) of pets who share your home.

1 BIRD
2 BIRDS
3 BIRDS
4 BIRDS
1 CAT

3 CATS
4 CATS

2 DOGS
3 DOGS
4 DOGS
1 FERRET
2 FERRETS
3 FERRETS
4 FERRETS

2 GUINEA PIGS
3 GUINEA PIGS
4 GUINEA PIGS
1 HAMSTER
2 HAMSTERS
3 HAMSTERS
4 HAMSTERS
1 RABBIT
2 RABBITS
3 RABBITS
4 RABBITS
1 REPTILE
2 REPTILES
3 REPTILES
4 REPTILES

1 GUINEA PIG

1 DOG

2 CATS

HELP RESCUE PETS!

that we mightn't otherwise want to have around if we didn't like the way they looked.

As for the door itself, if it's not made of metal, you may have to reinforce it. When we spent the first weekend in our new country house and left our pets alone there for the first time to run an errand, our dog Sam experienced an extreme case of separation anxiety, nearly succeeding in clawing his way through the turn-of-the-century wooden front door. If you have a pet with separation issues, put a sheet of protective diamond plate over the bottom half of the front door (as we did). As for cabinetry, many pets are adept at opening low doors to get at what's inside. If your dog likes to go hunting for interesting new property of yours to chew on, animal trainer Bill Berloni strongly recommends installing your cabinetry high out of reach of curious paws and teeth.

Your home is a haven for your animals, but as we saw in our tour of the kitchen, it's not without its hazards. A truly stylish animal house evicts all potential pet dangers from every single room.

Try this for an experiment: Get down on the floor to approximately the eye level of your pet. Then try to envision your place from his or her point of view. Treacherous passages can lurk in a home that hasn't been designed with pets in mind: That coffee table with a wrought-iron base might have ornamental curlicues ending in perilously sharp points. A glass-topped table can have equally dangerous corners. One plastic bag accidentally left lying around can get tangled around a cat's neck, with disastrous consequences. Electrical wires can kill if left where puppies, kittens, and rabbits can gnaw at them. Animal houses should banish insecticide trays, which could be mistaken for chew toys. Invisible fumes from a neighbor's extermination can seriously harm your bird, so if you're an apartment dweller, determine when pest control takes place in your building and make arrangements to evacuate your feathered friend.

If you're preparing to welcome an animal into your home, pretend for a few hours that you're the pet and make any necessary adjustments, such as cutting the looped handles of plastic bags so they don't accidentally become nooses for small, playful animals and coating electrical wires with a taste deterrent recommended by your local pet-supply store. While you're over by the electrical outlets, think of this: Your cat may see just fine in the dark — but you probably can't. Cats, especially playful kittens, have a way of always getting underfoot. Avoid stepping on, tripping over, or accidentally kicking your small pets by investing in a few good night-lights, such as Austin Innovations' Indiglo, which stays cool, lies flat against the electrical outlet, and is extremely safe for pets because it has no breakable glass parts. Plus, unlike most night-lights, which are tacky, the Indiglo looks modern and chic.

If your new pet is small (a cat, toy dog, ferret, or rabbit), be sure to outfit your windows with screens. We've seen the intriguing ways pet lovers live with art. For our pets, however, the most compelling vista isn't surrounded by a picture frame. It's the one they see through the window, which affords them a picture that changes from minute to minute. Rare is the pet who doesn't enjoy gazing out the window at passing insects, birds, and airplanes. But an open window poses a serious hazard, especially if you live on a high floor in an apartment building. In fact, the tragic phenomenon of pets falling to their death is so common it has a name: high-rise syndrome. No animal house should be without window screens; childproof window gates will not ensure your pets' safety, as smaller animals can slip through the bars.

Many cats like to sit right up against the screen, and twelve pounds of cat can easily push a flimsy screen right out of the window, so be sure to use well-made screens that fit snugly into the window frames. My favorite screens are called Window Filters, manufactured by R.E.P. Industries in Lansdale, Pennsylvania. They come equipped with strong rubber baffles for a safe, snug fit; warp-proof, rust-proof aluminum frames; and a filter that keeps out dust, dirt, and — dig this — 92 percent of ragweed pollen! Of course, screens also keep out those other pests: mosquitoes, flies, and hornets, whose stings are as bothersome to our pets as they are to us.

As for how you frame your windows — namely, window treatments — steer clear of elaborate curtains, drapery, and valances. If you just can't live without something hanging from a curtain rod, avoid delicate lace panels and gauzy sheers in favor of sturdy linen curtains that can be washed as often as necessary. For the window in my pit bulls' wag room, I opted for simple Ultrasuede curtains that relinquish pet hairs easily and can be thrown in the laundry whenever the occasion demands. Like any other fabric in an animal house, curtains are magnets for dust and pet hairs, only in this case it's all compounded by the outdoor dirt that naturally collects around the window area. Simple, attractive blinds, roller shades, Roman shades, or wooden shutters are the ticket for an animal house, especially a home with cats. With fabric shades, remember to pass your Helmac Tacky Vac or high-powered vacuum cleaner over them to keep them as dust- and hair-free as possible.

If you have a tendency to leave things lying about, now is the time to turn over a new leaf. Keep all potential chewables well out of reach of prying paws, especially bottles of medicine (if ingested by pets, many human medications are deadly). Ferrets are especially expert at hunting and gathering objects and hoarding them, so if you value your house keys, jewelry, sunglasses, cell phone, and TV remote, keep them in a safe place out of reach. Also, avoid reclining chairs, which can be deadly to ferrets, who have been known to get trapped in the mechanism and crushed.

In summer, make sure your swimming pool is covered, so your pets won't accidentally drown. In winter, if you need to use ice melt to clear your driveway, take care to use an animal-friendly brand such as Safe Paws that won't burn your dog's paw pads.

148

If your pet is blind or losing sight due to advanced age, avoid moving the furniture around. According to ophthalmologist Dr. Sandra van der Woerdt of the Animal Medical Center in New York, blind animals have the layout of your rooms "mapped out in their heads." So be considerate of your friends who have trouble seeing; don't go changing the furniture too often, or you'll confuse them and they'll wind up bumping into things and hurting themselves.

Renowned author, columnist, and home-keeping guru Heloise, who shares her Texas home with three dogs and a macaw, told me an inspiring story about her miniature schnauzer, Savvi, who recently went blind as a result of diabetes. Not wanting their beloved pet to be denied quality outdoor time and the freedom to come and go, she and her husband, David, devised an ingenious solution. David designed and built a private outdoor dog-run adjacent to their house. Indoors, in the living room, he constructed a carpeted tunnel-ramp that, like a funnel, starts out wide and gets narrower as it nears the wall. ("It's like a cattle chute," Heloise says.) After Heloise spritzed her signature perfume — Estée Lauder Private Collection — on the flap that leads outside, Savvi knew to follow her nose straight through the tunnel until she reached the door flap. Brilliant!

Above: Harry won't accidentally drown in Paul Donaher's swimming pool, thanks to a pool cover whose manufacturer claims it can support an elephant.

Some felines love nothing more than rooting around in potted plants. Although there are many unsightly ways to protect plants from being unearthed by digging paws (laying wire mesh over the soil is one), it's much more stylish to try the lovely and highly efficient method of spiking the soil with seashells, pinecones, or rocks. If Kitty can't get a toehold on the soft soil, she won't be inclined to pull up your roots. What's more, decorating the soil this way actually enhances the look of your plants without harming them in any way. Some people are as serious about their greenery as they are about pets, spending big bucks on plants, cachepots, and other accessories. I've heard tell of frustrated plant lovers dumping cats at shelters because they dug in the plants. That is not a stylish solution. If it's a contest between your plants and your pet, please find a new home for the plants; cats are not disposable.

Sometimes, it's pets that need protection from plants. Certain kinds of flora — like lilies — are poisonous to cats. "The plants you want to stay away from are diffenbachia and bulb plants, like tulips, amaryllis, and narcissus," explains Nina Humphrey of New York's Chelsea Garden Center. "Also keep cats away from avocado plants and fragrant geraniums." Planting simple wheat grass, Nina adds, is a good way to keep cats off of potentially harmful plants. "Cats crave green grass, so if you supply them with it, that'll prevent them from chewing or digging in your other plants." If you're not certain about which species of plant life are harmful to cats, consult your vet.

Design is important; if we don't like the way a product looks, we won't want to keep it around. That goes double for pet products. If our pets' paraphernalia — bedding, toys, and so forth — doesn't look good, we won't want it in our home. And that can have serious consequences for an animal house.

Pet toys are more than playthings; they're behavorial tools. An energetic dog requires a chew bone that will keep his attention from straying to your furniture. A cat needs a scratching post to keep his claws busy. Think of these "toys" as furniture insurance to keep the paws, jaws, and claws gainfully occupied — and away from your prized possessions.

Until recently, the pet industry came up short on the design front. But in the last few years, aesthetically oriented animal lovers have noticed an interesting trend: Visionary companies have started seeing fit to apply high design to products for pets. The ultimate proof that high design and pet products have finally met nose to nose? George, a San Francisco–based company named after the

Above: Landscape your plants' soil with polished river stones, and Kitty will quickly lose interest.

Right: A few artfully placed pinecones can ensure that flora will thrive even in a home with cats. This palm tree has grown to be seven feet tall!

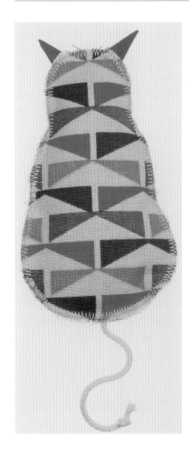

founders' wire-haired fox terrier, introduced the Wright On! catnip toy, fashioned of vintage Frank Lloyd Wright fabric and filled with organic catnip.

Nobody likes to look down at the living-room floor and see sanctioned chewables that look like something a prehistoric creature dragged in. Barbecue-brown rawhide bones and pigs' ears not only look unattractively unevolved, they are guaranteed to leave behind unwanted stains — and hickory-pit smells — as they're dragged to and fro by your beast. Plus, as Todd Oldham wisely points out, "they're nitrate-soaked extravaganzas that can't be healthy for our pets."

Fortunately, we now have an array of options that perform well, look good, and don't leave behind a smelly, unsightly mess. These include rubber toys such as the Kong and the Super-Tuff Rhino (which has a special place in my heart because the label says it's "pit bull tested" — and how!). If you prefer your dog toys to look like cubist artworks sculpted by Braque or Léger, fetch one or more of Blue Ribbon Dog Company's pure gum rubber Abstract dog bones or Surreal Sticks. Any one or all of these look splendid lying on the floor.

For cats, the range of attractive play outlets is still sadly limited, the Wright On! catnip toy notwithstanding. Cat scratchers are either covered in no-frills sisal or they're smothered in hideous nylon carpeting, in offensive office-furniture colors no design-conscious person would dream of displaying at home. And that's a big problem, because cats have an instinctive need to flex their claws — and if we fail to provide them with an outlet for this natural behavior, they will logically substitute our furni-

ture. That's why many Americans opt to declaw their feline friends. It's appalling that so many people have no problem mutilating cats' paws simply to preserve their furniture. The Clintons set a terrible example when they had Socks declawed *after* he'd spent seven long years in the animal house at 1600 Pennsylvania Avenue. Had someone thought to give Socks a decent scratching post, such a politically incorrect move might easily have been avoided.

Currently, we can count on one paw the good-looking cat scratchers available on the market: one by the San Francisco–based George that doubles as a kitty toy chest, another by Karate Kat, and the extra-tall Tiger Post from Angelical Cat Company. (A company called JoRene also offers the option of custom-covering their cat scratchers with your choice of carpet.) No wonder so many cat lovers prefer to just buy inexpensive sisal rugs and let Kitty do a number on them. Pricewise, these rugs compare favorably to underdesigned cat scratchers, and they hold Kitty's interest a lot longer.

One alternative to the meager offerings on the market is to improvise. Drooling over the Room catalog one evening, I came across a fantastic object: a metal vase covered in brown rope. I thought it might make a wonder-

ful alternative to the typical cat scratcher — and at $140 it was exactly the same price as one I'd seen at a pet-supply store. So I ordered one, arranged some flowers in it, weighted the bottom, and rubbed organic catnip on the outside to let the cats know it was okay for them to go for it. (Another alternative: If your home has stairs, wrap part of the banister with sisal twine from the hardware store, taking care to use only natural twine that has not been chemically treated with insecticides and the like.)

Believe it or not, the scratchers cats seem to love best — even my Scalamandré-loving connoisseurs — are not much to look at: They're rectangular blocks of humble, earth-friendly, recyclable corrugated cardboard that sit on the floor. Even when they're not scratching them, my cats love to hang out on them; something about that cardboard just feels good. The renowned architect Frank O. Gehry is famous for having designed corrugated furniture for Vitra back in the seventies that's still coveted to this day. Obviously, cat lovers shouldn't invest in furnishings made of tempting corrugated cardboard, rattan, or wicker. But why shouldn't cats have cardboard furniture of their own? Elizabeth Paige Smith of EPS Design in Los Angeles designs beautiful furniture for humans, including a few cardboard styles, and her collection includes a wonderful item created especially for felines: the Kitty Pod, a delightfully cozy circular perch that cats love to curl up in. So why shouldn't there be a corrugated cat scratcher worthy of an animal house that values good design, a feline toy that rises up from the floor like a sculptural monument, giving pleasure to humans and kittens alike? That's the question I posed to industrial designer Harry Allen — and he responded by inventing the most elegant cat scratcher I've ever seen.

If cats are given their own toys, they'll be much less likely to pounce on and paw at your beloved objects. Then again, there are cats who don't bother with tchotchkes. My friend Charlotte Barnard has delightful stories to tell about her two feline Fred Astaires, Pee Wee and Bingo, and how they gingerly walk about among her prized collection of antique salt and pepper shakers without breaking a one. The coffee table in Hunt Slonem's pink room is laden with breakables, including seashells and tall Venetian-glass vessels. Miraculously, Kitu the Abyssinian cat manages to avoid breaking a single thing, even though it's all out there

in the open. James Fairfax's cool cat, Silly, never disturbs the impressive examples of lusterware James has amassed; the collection is displayed on low, open shelves in his kitchen, where it survives unharmed. James's client Wendy Kershen manages to keep a splendid vase of flowers on her coffee table mere inches away from Quentin, her boisterous Boston terrier. How does she prevent accidents? By arranging her

Left: Teach your cat where to scratch by rubbing the surface with catnip and showing him how. This will help discourage him from trashing the objects and surfaces you treasure.

Below left: Inspired by the nesting instincts of her orange tabby, Simon, Elizabeth Paige Smith designed the Kitty Pod. Cats and their humans agree: It's out of this world.

Below right: This claw-shaped scratcher is the brainchild of Harry Allen — and it's a witty, sculptural piece of cat furniture that could spare a lot of felines from the declawing procedure.

flowers in a stylish vase from the Terence Conran Shop that's made of . . . white rubber! That way, if Quentin knocks down the vase, the worst that can happen is a water spill.

Most pet lovers are not knickknack fanciers; breakables often wind up dashed to the floor by our exuberant friends, who don't comprehend our strange attachment to these dust suckers. Frankly, I think our friends are onto something. Gathering dust does seem to be the knickknack's prime purpose, and dust is no friend to pets or humans. If you must have breakables lying about, be sure to position them high enough out of reach that they can survive unharmed. Fashion designer Stephen di Geronimo's apartment fairly overflows with beautiful antique decorative objets. But Pepe, Stephen's adorable Maltese, is too short to reach them. Cats, on the other hand, are arboreal, so

Right: Don't try this at home: Kitu the cat in the breakables-laden pink room at Hunt Slonem's.

156

they can climb ever higher and higher. When living with cats, the safest bet is to sell your breakables, give them away, or display them in cabinets behind glass.

Fragile objects displayed on low surfaces are definitely not advisable for animal houses. The suave shoe designer Warren Edwards lets two bossy females, Nicky and Nora, walk all over him and his possessions. He doesn't mind having the wall-to-wall carpeting professionally cleaned four times a year, but he draws the line at his art collection. His treasured objects include a couple of paintings in wood frames (chewable) and a vase of tulips (fragile; spills also cause damage to wood). The vase is delicately balanced on a wooden Tibetan monk's thong (highly chewable). How to guard all this from a pair of fiendishly clever wire-hair fox terriers? By placing the objects on a Biedermeier chest . . . and drawing the two coordinating side chairs just out of paw's reach.

For those who want the decoration of a breakable without the stress, Domus Design Collection offers a wonderful solution. The stunning 1060 coffee table by Draenert comes with a shell-shaped fossil carved by Mother Nature into its stone top. Obviously, a real shell is a fleeting, delicate item, but a shell's imprint endures for millennia. This understated, exquisitely sculptural table design offers the natural decorative beauty of a fragile object without the hassle of worrying whether or when it might fall and break.

Above left: Quentin relaxes at home, mere inches away from an arrangement of tulips and roses in a white vase that's guaranteed not to break because it's made of rubber.

Above right: Foiled again! In a scene right out of *The Thin Man,* Nicky and Nora can't quite reach their goal.

Above: The 1060 coffee table by Draenert is an elegant addition to any animal house.

Below: Stash your laundry safely away from prying jaws, paws, and claws.

In my pit bulls' wag room are two pine Table Lamps by Blu Dot. The lamp is actually attached to the table by a metal tube that continues down to form one leg of the table. In other words, it can't be toppled by the energetic tail thumping that frequently takes place in that room. (Incidentally, the lamp shade is made of flexible, translucent white plastic, a close cousin of the material used to make "E-collars," the lamp-shade contraptions that veterinarians use to prevent pets from bugging wounds that need to heal undisturbed. How's that for an appropriate wag-room accessory?)

If, like me, you're a bookworm who loves to collect old volumes, I'm here to tell you that you'll need to protect your pages from your pets. The delightfully sweet, musty smell of aged, yellowed, crumbling paper — whether it's paper- or hardbound, covered in linen or leather — is one of the most attractive aromas to cats and dogs, who will chew, shred, tear, and otherwise devour your treasured reading material. Just ask Christopher Brosius, who loves the scent so much he replicated it and added Paperback to the Demeter Fragrance Library. "The worst thing Zephyr ever did was my fault," Christopher recalls. "When he was still a puppy, I left a 1927 first edition of one of my favorite novels by Compton McKenzie on a low table. It was scarcer than hen's teeth. But when you live with a dog, you have to plan on these things."

Upon finishing the story of how his pups had devoured Turgenev and Dickens by the end of their first week in his home, Joe Dolce proudly remarks, "They have excellent taste." If people and their pets start to look alike, pets have an uncanny knack for developing a taste for our favorite reading matter. So it's only appropriate that the first books my cats made short work of were by Faulkner and Steinbeck. Birds are power chewers too, able to rip through wood with ease. And wouldn't you know, they find even *new* books appealing.

Evidently impressed that her favorite novelist, Sheri Holman, puts a green parrot in every book she writes ("It's my little Hitchcockian thing," Sheri explains), Ibrahim the mustache parakeet signals her approval by chewing the covers off any of Sheri's hardbound books she can get her feet on.

Pet-proofing must extend to the closet. Clothing and accessories — especially shoes, belts, and anything else made of leather — are very palatable to dogs and sometimes cats too, particularly, it seems, if they were made by Gucci, Prada, Hermès, Louis Vuitton, Chanel, or Coach. It's up to you to be sure these items stay safely out of reach of curious paws and teeth. Way out of reach. (If your dogs, like mine, are known leash chompers, keep the leashes hanging high out of their reach too — especially if the leashes in question are, like your shoes, by Gucci, Prada, Hermès . . .) One of my dogs is the canine counterpart of Inspector Gadget; she's particularly adept at reaching into out-of-the-way places and pulling out whatever her heart desires, and what her heart desires usually bears a Coach label. Plastic storage bins are fine provided your dog isn't a proven power chewer. I've heard of dogs who've been known to crush unopened cans of dog food — what chance could an innocent little Sterilite box have against jaw power like that? You may even wish to consult a professional closet organizer, such as California Closets, to help maintain order.

It's a good idea to look out for your laundry too. Dogs love nesting in our soiled laundry because, well, it smells like the people who wore it (i.e., us). But sometimes our pets will do more than just nest with laundry; they'll start nibbling at it, tearing off buttons, even shredding sheets and towels (yes, I've had this happen to me). Devise an attractive hamper or basket arrangement and take care not to leave soiled laundry lying about.

It's all the rage nowadays for people to take their shoes off before entering their own or other people's homes. Not long ago, it was considered odd or even impolite to ask visitors to doff their footwear before coming inside your home. These days, however, it's a bona fide trend in the most stylish homes; some hosts even provide slippers for their guests. It makes sense: Why make cleanup harder? Taking one's shoes off automatically puts one at ease and makes one feel at home. Again, it's just a matter of changing our perspective. At my place, inspired by my

Below: Sign of the times: Friendly messages like these have replaced the "Beware of Dog" warnings of yore.

CLOSE GATE
DOGS AT PLAY

friends Beth and Hideaki, I encourage shoe removal. Hideaki is from Japan, where shoe removal is customary. So imagine how mortified I was when he and Beth came over for dinner with their son Osamu, Hideaki removed his footwear, and upon finishing dinner, I discovered that one of my dogs had chewed my guest's shoes! To make sure this never happens again, we've installed metal shelving by our front door, placed high enough that the dogs can't reach it. Once again, necessity was the mother of a pretty nifty invention at my animal house.

Having your Pradas pawed, clawed, or otherwise mauled can cause more than just frustration and frantic calls to the purchase protection division of American Express. Imagine the heartbreak of the woman whose dog devoured a pair of expensive velvet loafers. Pricy as they were, those shoes had a terrible hidden cost: After the dog had ingested the velvet scraps, they somehow became sharper than glass, slicing his intestinal tract. After several painful surgeries, the dog died. That is a sad, true story. And if it can't convince you to put away your belongings, I don't know what can.

The good news is that every day, more and more pet lovers are taking simple — and simply chic — steps to ensure their animals' safety.

Visitors to the ancient city of Pompeii can see an early example of animal-house signage that survived the awesome destruction wreaked by Mount Vesuvius's eruption. The sign takes the form of a mosaic depicting a menacing dog alongside the legend "*Cave Canem*" — Latin for "Beware of Dog." That same warning appears on every doghouse in every Looney Tunes cartoon with a mean-looking bulldog in it.

Once upon a time, dogs' main purpose was to guard our homes. Now, grateful for all the other wonderful ways they've enhanced our lives, we take care to look out for them. Today's typical animal-house warning is more likely to deliver a message that's a lot fuzzier — like the handmade sign greeting visitors to Paul Donaher's Hamptons home. It reads, "Close Gate — Dogs at Play." Signs like this send a message that clearly comes from a place of love.

And isn't that what an animal house is?

ACKNOWLEDGMENTS

*S*o many amazing humans and animals touched this book that completing it felt more like play than work. With admiration and gratitude, I offer thanks to . . .

Jessica Wainwright, sister, motivator, friend—more than an agent to me; Joseph Montebello for believing; Carol Judy Leslie and my brilliant editor, Karen "The Great" Dane, of Bulfinch Press for adopting this book and parenting it; Martha and George Szabo for parenting me, a dog named Bodri, and two foundling cats; Frank Andrews for encouraging me to write a book; Mary Tyler Moore for making my day; Bash Dibra for the three Ps (Patience, Perseverance, and Praise) and for training me to think like a beast; Brad Hamilton for inspirational editing ("Well, here's your box"); Matthew Morris for being the embodiment of animal house style; Dennis Golonka for sharing his Rolodex; Harry Allen for surpassing my vision of the world's first cat-scratcher-as-monument; Tim Convery for a fierce emergency sticker; Wendy Medina and Patricia Wehman of Toray Ultrasuede for their early and continued support; Todd Oldham for the cherished gift of his trust; Kathy Bauch of the Humane Society of the United States for too many kindnesses to list here . . .

Carolina Herrera, Michael Maharam, Deborah Hughes, Seemak Hakakian, Anna-Sophia Leone, Paola Antonelli, Seen Lippert, Christopher Brosius, Robin Bell Schaefer, Laren Stover, Lisa Silhanek, Conn Brattain, Colleen Curtis, and Kazuko for astonishing purity of heart—I am so glad to know you! . . .

Everyone who so graciously gave access—you are the heart and soul of this book: Chris Madden, Eleanor Mondale, Paul Mansour, Lisa Fine, Michael Davis, Joe Dolce, Jonathan Burnham, Charlotte Frieze, Hunt Slonem, Robin Elmslie Osler, Bruce Matthews, Gabriele Sanders, Timmy Haskell, Harold Koda, George Lynch, Victor Tolintino, Shannon McLean, Kim Vernon, Elizabeth Lippman, Jean-Claude Huon, Han Feng, Michael Levinson, Ken Eichler, Leslie Simitch, Faith Popcorn (it's an honor to be on your TalentBank!), Richard Lambertson, John Truex, Amy Kizer, George

Malkemus, Tony Yurgaitis, James Fairfax, Wendy Kershen, Dennis Lee, Tony Esposito, Gigi Green, Joan Wren, Ann Wren, Elizabeth Paige Smith, Clodagh, Linda Lambert, Simon Doonan, Jonathan Adler, Stephen Miller Siegel, Barbara Taylor Bradford, Victoria Mackenzie-Childs, Mark Welsh, John Bartlett, Marco Maccioni, Sheila Bridges, Peter Vaughn, Anya Larkin, Sheri Holman, Christine Butler, Warren Edwards, Robert Marc, Bill Roach, James Blauvelt, Paul Donaher, Mary and Eric Shefferman, Spalding Gray, Kathie Russo, Carlton Davis, Anita Monteith, Christina Grajales, Isabelle Kirshner, Kohle Yohannan, James Gager, Sandi Schneider, Arden and Daryl Dewbrey, Randall and Connie Jones, Erica Lennard, Denis Colomb, Fredrick Fragasso, Stephen Hammond, Kate Spade, Kathy Bishop, Robert Homma, Stephen di Geronimo, Gary Kaskel, Laura Brown, Lori Tesoro, Jodi Richard, Anne and Tony Fisher, Chassie Post, Phil Costello, Michelle Star, David Piscuskas, David Raney . . .

All the wonderful people who are so generous with everything they know: Linda LaChapelle, Pandora Castelli, and Kemit "K.J." Johnson of LaChapelle Representation, Heloise, Seamus Leahy, Katherine Powis of the Horticultural Society of New York, Valerie Cates, Tom Sachs, Robert Verdi, Dennis Wedlick, Kelly Ann Heeralal, Karen Peterson, Jo Gibbs, Ellen Carey, Catriona Pike, Valerie McKenzie, Liat Margolis, Brier Tomlinson, Tomoko Shimura, Corin Angel, Griselda Perez, Judy Glick, Nina Humphrey of Chelsea Garden Center, Amy Crain, Dr. Peter Borchelt, Rebecca "Dr. Becky" Campbell, Torkan, Ron Nemec, Charlotte Barnard, Stephanie Mauer, Bernadette Peters, Jeffrey Steingarten, Gail Simmons, Cynthia Cathcart, Florence Palomo, Sandra DeFeo and Bill Berloni of the Humane Society of New York, Stacey Shub of FIDONYC, Beth Terry, Rosaly Grunberg, Dr. Julie Butler, Marilyn Blohm of the Center for Animal Care & Control, Special Agent Annemarie Lucas and Valerie Angeli of the ASPCA, Dr. Sandra van der Woerdt, Dr. Karen Aiken and Beth Lambert of the Animal Medical Center, Dr. Stanley Coren, Dr. Joel Gold, Julie Sheridan, Quintana Dunne, Heather Messer, R. D. Chin, Stephen Learner, Mary Murphy, Andrew Page, Laura Resen, Lizzie Himmel, Diane Lewis, Susan Penzner, Bill Leonard, Nancy Holmes, Susan Grant Lewin, Diane Villani, Marisa Acocella, Andrea Arden, Fay Duftler, Choire Sicha, Karen Mauersberg, Paul Armstrong, Diane Weisenberg, Tim Ousey, Glenn Davish, Matthew Smyth, Carmen Ramos Cruz and Irene Quinn of St. Francis de Sales Church, Kay Mann, Jeffrey Roth, Stephan Valter, Dana Gioia . . .

Marian McEvoy for her great style and humanity (and for giving me the pass key to so many chic animal houses!) and everyone on her *House Beautiful* team, especially Regina Clarbour, Nora Sheehan, Senga Mortimer, Elaine Greene, and Betsy Hunter . . .

The people who came through for me in a serious way: Mary Jones and Nicola Corl of Ultra, Christopher Bailey, Theresa Zajkowski, Bernice Kwok-Gabel, Michele Nicoll . . .

The team at Bulfinch Press, especially eagle-eyed copyeditor Betsy Uhrig for her incredible attention to detail, Bruce Campbell for his kick-ass book design, and Melissa Langen in production for sheepdogging the whole thing through . . .

The awesome Stan Wan, a.k.a. Lone Wolf (where have you been all my life?), and the other photographers whose beautiful images grace these pages: John Gilliland and his team (Scott Grayland, Annie Schlechter, Julie Verrona), Greg Broom, Pascal Blancon (and Tom Maher), Ivan Terestchenko, Antoine Bootz, Joachim Magrean, Dirk Westphal, Horace Long, Lynn Campbell, Dan Forer, Micheline Pelletier/Corbis Sygma, Peter Aaron/Esto, Jeff Goldberg/Esto, Mark Platt . . .

The makeup artists who made every day a good hair day: Carmel Bianco and MiRa of Link, Bata Plavsik, Craig van den Brulle, Donald Simrock, Carol Ann of Dandie . . .

The talented Rob Southern for cheerfully consulting on the redesign of the ever-evolving American pit bull terrier living room (a.k.a. wag room); Mackenzie Pierson for an inspiring paint job; Camille Casaretti for couture-quality slipcovers; Prudence Designs for the most captivating floral arrangements known to man or beast . . .

The Center for Animal Care & Control and Delaware Valley Humane Society for entrusting me with the loves of my life . . .

The great teachers (wish you were here): Dean T. Mace, Linda Krimsley Lechner, Leo Lerman, Liz Tilberis, Richard Martin, Roger Caras, Darwin, Pakorn, and Sissi . . .

And John Maher, for driving the Volvo, taste-testing the kibble, and coining a little phrase, "dog-as-furniture," that really got me thinking.

RESOURCE GUIDE

FOREWORD

Page 7: For information about the Humane Society of the United States in Washington, D.C., and its programs, contact 202-452-1100 or go to www.hsus.org

1. WELCOME

Page 13: For information about the Delta Society in Rinton, WA, contact 425-226-7357 or go to www.deltasociety.org; page 15: Baker Furniture, NYC, 212-725-5175 or www.bakerfurniture.com; Home Depot, 800-553-3199 or www.homedepot.com; Marvin Windows and Doors, 800-373-0087 or www.marvin.com; Kroin, 800-OK-KROIN or www.kroin.com; Mitchell Gold Furniture Co., 800-789-5401 or www.mitchellgold.com; page 16: La Mesa straw rug from Aleman Moore, 718-349-8221; Humane Society of New York, NYC, 212-752-4842 or www.humanesociety.org; Donghia, 800-DONGHIA; Todd Hase, 212-334-3568; Christian Liaigre to the trade from Holly Hunt, 800-229-8559; rug by Veedon Fleece 011-44-148-357-5758 or www.veedonfleece.demon.co.uk; Anya Larkin Ltd., 212-532-3263; page 18: furniture by LeCorbusier available at Cassina USA, 212-245-2121 or www.cassina-usa.com; page 19: Bodo Sperlein white bowl vase to order from Lille, Chicago, 773-342-0563; page 20: *Elle Decor* subscriptions, 850-682-7654; page 21: white cotton slipcovers by Camille Casaretti Custom Interiors, Brooklyn, NY, 718-875-3111; page 22: vintage Jens Risom sofa from Swank 20th Century Modern, 212-673-8597, and new Jens Risom lounge chairs from Knoll, NYC, 212-343-4000 or www.knoll.com; page 23: arrangement by Prudence Designs, NYC, 212-691-1541; Alvar Aalto vase by Iitala from the Museum of Modern Art Design Store, 212-767-1050 or www.moma-store.org (for more stores: 800-448-8252); West Highland chair by Chris Madden from Bassett Furniture (for stores: 540-629-6000 or www.bassettfurniture.com); page 24: *Interior Design* subscriptions, 800-900-0804; *Nest* subscriptions, 212-639-9163; furniture by Pierre Paulin available at Totem Design, 212-925-5506 or www.totemdesign.com, and Möbelform, 888-662-3546 or www.mobelform.com; page 25: Catoe & Bambu, 212-713-1502; Tails in Need, 212-327-3164 or www.tailsin-

need.com; *Country Living* subscriptions, 800-337-2502; Neptune Rug by Denis Colomb from Homer, 212-744-7705 or www.homerdesign.com; page 26: Animal Rescue Fund (A.R.F.), 631-537-0400; East Quogue Animal Shelter, 631-635-5900; seagrass carpet (sold by the square foot, then bound) from Linoleum City, Los Angeles, CA, 323-469-0063; page 27: for information about the San Francisco SPCA Open Door Program, 415-554-3098 or www.sfspca.org; the Corcoran Group, NYC, 212-355-3550 or www.corcoran.com

2. CRITTER COMFORTS

Page 29: Pet Hair Pic-Up from Lechter's, 800-326-1376 or www. lechters.com (for more stores: 800-435-6223 or www.evercare.com); page 30: Apron rug by Diane Elson, Wave sofa by Giovanni Offredi, and 927 table by Mauro Lipparini from Saporiti Italia at Domus Design Collection, 212-685-0800 or www.ddcnyc.com; page 31: Dolce Vita chaise by Pascal Mourgue from Ligne Roset, NYC, 800-BYROSET or www.ligne-roset.com; Plush Jack squeaky tug toy by J&Y Pet Products from Petco, 888-583-6044 or www.petco.com; yellow Planet Kong Xtreme Goodie Ship (on chaise) from Dogtoys.com (for more stores: 303-216-2626 or www.kongcompany.com); page 32: butterfly chair from Crate & Barrel, 800-717-1112 or www.crateandbarrel.com; Circular Chair and Baby Circular Chair by Lampa, 631-722-9450 or www.lampa.com; Felt-Up Chair by Blu Dot available at Ad Hoc, NYC, 212-982-7703 (for more stores, or catalog: 612-782-1844 or www.bludot.com); page 33: leopard fabric to the trade from Scalamandré, NYC, 800-932-4361; page 34: to contact Out of the Pits, e-mail out_of_the_pits@hotmail.com; page 35: *Elle* subscriptions, 800-876-8775; North Shore Animal League, Port Washington, NY, 516-883-7575; Missoni, NYC, 212-517-9339; Animal Rescue Fund (A.R.F.), Wainscott, NY, 631-537-0400; page 36: Sun and Moon Originals cushion from East West Books, NYC, 212-243-5994 (for more stores: 800-775-8639); Marcel Wanders Shadow Lamp from Cappellini Modern Age, NYC, 212-966-0669; rubber mat from Restoration Hardware, 800-762-1005 or www.RestorationHardware.com; page 37: floor cushion by Pottery Barn, 800-922-9934 or www.potterybarn.com; cat bed from Martha By Mail, 800-950-7130 or www.marthabymail.com; Angela Adams pillows available at Barney's, 212-826-8900 (for more stores, 800-255-9454 or go to www.angelaadams.com); floor pillow from Mitchell Gold Furniture Co., 800-789-5401 or www.mitchellgold.com; page 38: Low Lounger by Eazy Bean from Karikter, NYC, 212-274-1966 (for more stores, 415-255-8516); camouflage slipcovers by Camille Casaretti Custom Interiors, Brooklyn, NY, 718-875-3111; page 39: pillows and pottery from Jonathan Adler, NYC, 212-941-8950, and East Hampton, NY, 631-329-6499; Greysland Greyhound Adoption, 508-435-6023; vintage Heywood-Wakefield furniture from City Barn Antiques, NYC,

212-941-5757; page 40: fabric to the trade from Clarence House, 212-752-2890 or 800-632-0076; Snuggaluvs white dog bed with black piping from Fetch, NYC, 212-352-8591 (for more stores: 323-851-3070); *House & Garden* subscriptions, 800-234-1520; page 41: Albrizzi Design, NYC, 212-570-0417; Rose Cumming Inc., NYC, 212-758-0844; page 42: sofa and ottoman from Henredon, 800-444-3682 or www.henredon.com; rug from Tufenkian Design, NYC, 800-581-9266 or www.tufenkiancarpets.com; page 43: Swan chair by Arne Jacobsen from Knoll, NYC, 212-343-4000 or www.knoll.com

3. GET DOWN

Page 48: Pergo, 800-33-PERGO or www.pergo.com; Home Depot, 800-553-3199; Husky Hardwood Floors, 877-MILL-DIRect; Ralph Lauren paint colors (on floor) by Sherwin-Williams from Janovic Plaza, NYC, 800-772-4381 (for more stores: 888-881-0263); page 50: tiles from D&W Flooring, Denver, CO, 303-288-8898; dining chairs by Donghia, 800-DONGHIA; page 51: Armstrong, 800-233-3823, Dept. 610; page 53: seagrass carpet from Misha Carpet, NYC, 212-688-5912; page 54: Nature's Miracle products sold at Petco, 888-583-6044 or www.petco.com, and Petopia.com (for more stores: 310-544-7125); armchair covered in semi-antique Turkish kilim from George Smith, NYC, 212-226-4747 or www.georgesmith.com; birdcage by Hoei (for stores: 808-677-7749); page 55: Azari rug from ABC Carpet & Home, NYC, 212-473-3000; page 56: Einstein Moomjy, NYC, 212-758-0900; Pet-Agree, 800-BEST-BUY or www.pet-agree.com; Stark Carpet, NYC, 212-752-9000 or www.starkcarpet.com; page 57: Fiber-Seal, 800-TUFSEAL or www.fiberseal.com

4. FOUR WALLS, FOUR PAWS

Page 58: cage from King's Cages, 631-777-7300 or www. kingscages.com; page 60: wallpaper designs by Tyler Hall, NYC, 212-239-0362 or www.tyler-hall.com; Janovic Plaza, NYC, 800-772-4381; page 61: Ralph Lauren paint colors by Sherwin-Williams (for stores: 888-881-0263); Benjamin Moore chartreuse paint from Janovic Plaza, NYC, 800-772-4381 (for more stores: 800-344-0400); page 63: Eames Hang-It-All from the Museum of Modern Art Design Store, NYC, 212-767-1050 or www.moma-store.org (for more stores: 616-654-3000 or www.hermanmiller.com); artworks by Joe Andoe available at Joseph Helman Gallery, NYC, 212-245-2888; page 64: artworks by Martha Szabo available at www.marthaszabo.com; Doyle New York, NYC, 212-427-2730 or www.doylenewyork.com; page 65: artworks by George Rodrigue available at Rodrigue Gallery, New Orleans, LA, 504-581-4244 or www.bluedogart.com; Crayola eggshell interior latex paint in Buttercup from Janovic Plaza, NYC, 800-772-4381 (for more stores: 610-253-6271); page 66: artworks by Sue Coe available at the Galerie St.

Etienne, NYC, 212-245-6734 or www.artnet.com/etienne.html; artworks by Roy Kortick available at Debs & Co., NYC, 212-643-2070; artworks by Andrew Ehrenworth available at James Graham & Sons, NYC, 212-535-5767; page 67: Harry Barker Gallery, Savannah, Georgia, 912-527-2700 or www.harrybarker.com; page 67: artworks by Tillie available at www.tillamookcheddar.com; artworks by Norm Magnusson available at Bridgewater/Lustberg & Blumenfeld Gallery, NYC, 212-941-6355; page 68: artworks by Julian Opie available at Barbara Krakow Gallery, Boston, MA, 617-262-4490 or www. barbarakrakowgallery.com; Bionaire products from Gracious Home, NYC, 212-517-6300 (for more stores: 800-253-2764 or www.bion-aireproducts.com); page 69: for artworks by Steve Keene call 718-384-0661; new Eames wooden screen from the Museum of Modern Art Design Store, NYC, 212-767-1050 or www.momastore.org (for more stores: 616-654-3000 or www.hermanmiller.com); denim dog beds from L.L. Bean, Freeport, ME, 800-552-5437 or www.llbean.com; Yesterday's News Cat Litter from PetSmart, PetsWarehouse.com, and ThatPetPlace.com (for more stores: 800-267-5287); *Bird Talk* subscriptions, 800-365-4421 or www.birdtalk.com; *The Pet Bird Report* subscriptions, 877-650-1631 or www.petbird-report.com; G and L Architects, NYC, 212-962-1292; page 70: Fiesta bowls for dogs and cats from Sylvester's, Sag Harbor, NY, 631-725-5012; Fiesta tableware from Bloomingdale's, NYC, 212-705-2000 (for more stores: 304-387-1300); slub-velvet sofa from Laura Ashley, NYC, 212-496-5110; coffee table from the Bombay Co. (for stores: 800-829-7789 or www.bombayco.com); breakfast tray from Gracious Home, NYC, 212-517-6300; ARQ Architects, Kittery, ME, 207-439-5286 or www.ARQArchitects.com; Stephen Learner Studio Ltd., NYC, 212-741-8583; 1100 Architect, P.C., NYC, 212-645-1011; page 71: Ultrasuede by Toray Ultrasuede America, NYC, 212-382-1590 or www.ultrasuede.com; page 72: Dennis Wedlick, architect, 212-625-9222; brackets from Smith & Hawken, 800-981-9888; rope perch from Petco, 888-583-6044 or www.petco.com; page 73: alligators from McFeely's Square Drive Screws, Lynchburg, VA, 800-443-7937 or www.mcfeelys.com; page 75: Living Color Enterprises, Fort Lauderdale, FL, 800-878-9511 or www.livingcolor.com; Lucite fish tank by Fredrick's Aquatic Decor & Maintenance, NYC, 212-628-6770; Bang & Olufsen, 847-299-9380 or www.bang-olufsen.com

5. FETCHING FABRICS

Page 77: Pottery Barn, 800-922-9934 or www.potterybarn.com; Crate & Barrel, 800-717-1112 or www.crateandbarrel.com; Ikea, 800-434-4532 or www.ikea.com; Ethan Allen, Danbury, CT, 203-743-8481; page 78: TFP Design, 323-227-9777; vacuum cleaner by Miele, 800-843-7231 or www.mieleusa.com; Helmac Tacky Vac hand roller from Petco, 888-583-6044 or www.petco.com, and Lechter's, 800-326-1376 or

www.lechters.com (for more stores: 800-435-6223 or www.evercare.com); page 80: *House Beautiful* subscriptions, 800-444-6873; camouflage fabrics to order at Iceberg Army Navy of Soho, NYC, 212-226-8454; slipcovers by Camille Casaretti Custom Interiors, Brooklyn, NY, 718-875-3111; Ultrasuede throw by Jet Set Chat et Chien, 914-271-1146; woven sisal carpet by Beauvais Carpets, 212-688-2265; Abstract rubber bone and Torpedo ball by K9 Sport available at Fetch, 212-352-8591; page 81: Rogers & Goffigon fabrics to the trade from Rogers & Goffigon, NYC, 212-888-3242; Marimekko fabrics to the trade from Delgreco & Co., 212-688-5310; page 82: Lee Jofa fabrics to the trade from Lee Jofa, NYC, 212-688-0444; page 83: Maharam fabrics to the trade from Maharam, 800-645-3943 or www.maharam.com; Clarence House Bristol cotton to the trade from Clarence House, 212-752-2890; Cowtan & Tout fabrics to the trade from Cowtan & Tout, 212-647-6900; page 84: Ultrasuede from Toray Ultrasuede America, NYC, 212-382-1590 or www.ultrasuede.com; De Sede D5422 reclining chair from Domus Design Collection, NYC, 212-685-0800 or www.ddc-nyc.com; Throw-Away collection of furniture by Zanotta from Moss, NYC, 212-226-2190; vintage Heywood-Wakefield chair and sectional sofa from City Barn Antiques, NYC, 212-941-5757; Table Lamp from Blu Dot, Minneapolis, MN (for stores or catalog: 612-782-1844 or www.bludot.com); page 85: ottoman, sofa, and chairs by Le Décor Français, NYC, 212-734-0032; mohair by Old World Weavers, NYC, 212-355-7186; page 86: Maharam fabrics to the trade from Maharam, NYC, 800-645-3943 or www.maharam.com; page 87: Larsen fabrics to the trade from Cowtan & Tout, NYC, 212-647-6900; Sunbrella fabric by Glen Raven (for sources: 800-788-4413 or www.sunbrella.com); Ethan Allen, Danbury, CT, 203-743-8481; Pottery Barn, 800-922-9934 or www.potterybarn.com; Minotti leather and calf-hide sofas from SEE Ltd., NYC, 212-228-3600 or www.minotti.com; faux-fur throws by Bed, Bath & Beyond, 800-GO BEYOND or www.bedbathandbeyond.com, and Takashimaya, NYC, 212-350-0100; Mercer chair in British tan and red wool plaid blanket from Coach, NYC, 212-754-0041; page 88: vintage leather sofas from ABC Carpet & Home, NYC, 212-473-3000; dog leashes by Wagwear available at Fetch, NYC, 212-352-8591; De Sede leather sofas and chairs from Domus Design Collection, NYC, 212-685-0800 or www.ddcnyc.com; page 89: Zanotta Blow chair available at Moss, NYC, 212-226-2190; B&B Italia, NYC, 800-872-1697 or www.bebitalia.it

6. WHOSE BED IS IT, ANYWAY?

Page 91: To contact the Dachshund Friendship Club, write to 200 East 10th Street, Box 817, New York, NY 10003; page 92: for stores carrying Frette Home Couture, 212-299-0400; lavender-filled pillows by Beddy's Bed'n Art, 607-783-2647; Red Rover dog bed available at Fetch, 212-352-8591; page 93: K9 Sport performance bed from

the Terence Conran Shop, NYC, 212-755-9079 (for more stores: 212-736-9085); page 94: brocade fabrics from Harry Zarin Co., NYC, 212-925-6112; Posturepedic mattress by Sealy, 800-877-7496; Ralph Lauren Aragon leopard-print sheets from Polo Ralph Lauren, NYC, 212-606-2100 (also available at Bloomingdale's and Macy's); page 95: for an Ikea store near you, or to request a catalog, 800-434-4532 or www.ikea.com; Vellux blanket from Target, 800-800-8800; Vellux blankets and matelassé coverlets by Martha Stewart Everyday from Kmart, 800-866-0086; for a Company Store catalog, 800-285-3696; for a Chambers catalog, 800-334-9790; for a Garnet Hill catalog, 800-622-6216; Ultrasuede and cashmere sleeping bag from Troy, NYC, 212-941-4777; Pascal Mourgue bed from Ligne Roset, NYC, 800-BYROSET or www.ligne-roset.com; Flou Nathalie bed with cotton canvas cover from Garnet Hill, 800-622-6216 (for other Flou fabric options, including Ultrasuede, contact Domus Design Collection, NYC, 212-685-0800 or www.ddcnyc.com); page 96: wrought-iron bed from Charles P. Rogers Brass and Iron Bed Co., NYC, 212-675-4400 or www.charlesprogers.com; matelassé coverlet and shams from The Company Store (for catalog: 800-285-3696); page 99: Philipp Plein dog bed available at Möbelform, 888-662-3546 or www.mobelform.com; custom Plexiglas furniture to order at Plexi-Craft Quality Products Corp., NYC, 212-924-3244; page100: African Leopard fabric by Toray Ultrasuede, NYC, 212-382-1590 or www.ultrasuede.com; down-filled dog bed (monogramming available) from The Company Store, 800-285-3696 or www.thecompanystore.com; page 102: Snuggaluvs navy dog bed with white piping from Barkley, NYC, 212-734-9373 (for more stores: 323-851-3070); the Donut Bed by Bowsers Pet Products from Petco, 888-583-6044 or www.petco.com (for more stores: 877-BOWSERS or www.bowsers.com); machine-washable sheepskin throw from Ikea, 800-434-4532 or www.ikea.com; page 103: Snuggaluvs dog-eared, monogrammed bed from Fetch, NYC, 212-352-8591

7. SOMEONE'S IN THE KITCHEN WITH FIDO

Page 105: Sub-Zero, 800-222-7820 or www.subzero.com; Viking, 662-451-4133 or www.vikingrange.com; page 106: Chilewich Ray-Bowl from the Museum of Modern Art Design Store, NYC, 212-767-1050 or www.momastore.org (for more stores: 212-343-2969); page 108: bullet cans from Crate & Barrel, 800-717-1112 or www.crate-andbarrel.com; "cancan" canisters from Sherry-Lehmann, NYC, 212-838-7500; for stores carrying feed scoops by Little Giant Farm, Ranch and Pet Products, contact Miller Manufacturing Co., Eagan, MN, 800-260-0888; page 109: Blitz Pour & Store feed dispenser from Drs. Foster & Smith, 800-826-7206 or www.drsfostersmith.com; Emile Henry Burgundian clay cookware (shown in red and yellow) and rack from Sur La Table, Seattle, WA, 800-243-0852 or www.surlatable.com; All-Clad saucepan from

Macy's, NYC, 212-695-4400; page 110: Good Buddy Cookies from Castor & Pollux Pet Products, available at Kings, Big Y, and Draeger's (for more stores: 800-875-7518 or www.castorpolluxpet.com); page 111: Azmira, 800-497-5665 or www.Azmira.com; Canidae and Felidae, 800-398-1600 or www.canidae.com; Natura Pet (makers of Innova and California Natural), 800-532-7261 or www.naturapet.com; Old Mother Hubbard (makers of Wellness), 800-225-0904 or www.oldmotherhubbard.com; Solid Gold, 800-364-4863 or www.solidgoldhealth.com; Wysong, 517-631-0009 or www.wysong.net; Howlin' Gourmet dog treats from Dancing Paws available at Petco, 888-583-6044 or www.petco.com (for more stores: 888-644-PAWS or www.dancing-paws.com); Wedgwood jasperware dog and cat bowls by Nick Munro from Bloomingdale's, Dayton Hudson, Macy's, and Marshall Field's (for more stores: 800-677-7860 or www.wedgwood.com); New York Dog leather bone-shaped place mat from Barkley, NYC, 212-734-9373 (for more stores: 646-486-1331); page 112: Fiesta bowls for dogs and cats from Sylvester's, Sag Harbor, NY, 631-725-5012; place mat from Crate & Barrel, 800-717-1112 or www.crateandbarrel.com; page 113: Mackenzie-Childs tableware from Mackenzie-Childs, NYC, 212-570-6050 (also available at Neiman Marcus stores); Delilah Enterprises hand-painted banquet tables from Peter's Emporium for Pets, NYC, 212-772-3647 (for more stores: 505-286-2014); Sheila Parness lead-crystal and bone-china pet bowls from Bergdorf Goodman, NYC, 212-753-7300; Z-Spot, NYC, 212-472-4960; page 114: Teledyne Water Pik faucet filter, 800-525-2774 or www.waterpik.com; Robinson Ransbottom stoneware dog bowls from Restoration Hardware, 800-762-1005 or www.RestorationHardware.com; page 115: Robinson Ransbottom Dog and Kitty bowls to order from Robinson Ransbottom Pottery Co., Roseville, OH, 888-779-8868; page 116: K9 Sport bowl and Cordura nylon feed pad from the Terence Conran Shop, NYC, 212-755-9079; OXO computer cart from Kartell, NYC, 212-966-6665; page 117: Magis "Bombo" hydraulic stool from Ovale, Red Bank, NJ, 732-933-0437; metal bowls with rubber nonskid rings from Restoration Hardware, 800-762-1005 or www.RestorationHardware.com; Doris Day Animal League, 202-546-1761 or www.ddal.org

8. BATH TIME FOR BONZO

Page 118: scalloped bath linens by D. Porthault, NYC, 212-688-1660 or www.dporthault.fr; page 119: Pets Alive, Middletown, NY, 914-386-9738; page 120: Wee Wee Pads by Four Paws Pet Products from Petco, 888-583-6044 or www.petco.com (for more stores: 631-434-1100); chrome-plate towel bar from Pottery Barn, 800-922-9934 or www.potterybarn.com; tiles from Ideal Tile, NYC, 212-799-3600; page 124: Espree Hypoallergenic Shampoo from PetsMart (for more stores: 800-328-1317); Earthbath sold at Petco, 888-583-6044 or www.petco.com, and Pet Food

Express (for more stores: 415-771-1166 or www.earthbath.com); Oh My Dog! fragrance available at Sephora, 877-SEPHORA, and Saks Fifth Avenue, NYC, 212-753-4000 or www.saksfifthavenue.com; Aesop Animal shampoo available at Barneys, 212-826-8900; Origins Silky Coat dog shampoo from Origins stores, 800-ORIGINS; Fauna products available at Nordstrom's (for more stores: 800-536-1909); for inquiries about the Cateau by Brier Tomlinson, e-mail briertom@aol.com; Vicci litter box by United Pets, 011-3902-3927041 or www.unitedpets.it; for stores carrying World's Best Cat Litter, 877-367-9225 or www.worldsbestcatlitter.com; page 127: Recess bathroom accessory from Futura Distinctive Hardware, a division of Franklin Brass Mfg. Co., Dominguez, CA, 310-885-3200; By Bing Amazing Vase and Plastic Fantastic by Harry Gutfreund, both available at the Museum of Modern Art Design Store, NYC, 212-767-1050 or www.momastore.org; shower curtain from Pottery Barn, 800-922-9934 or www.potterybarn.com

9. UP TO SNIFF

Page 128: Midwest crate from R. C. Steele, 800-872-3777 or www.rcsteele.com; page 130: Miele, 800-843-7231 or www.mieleusa.com; for stores carrying the Dust Caesar, call 800-770-7894; page 133: for a free copy of People for the Ethical Treatment of Animals' Cruelty-Free Household Product Companies List and the Cruelty-Free Pocket Shopping Guide, 757-622-7382, ext. 442; Ecover sold at Whole Foods, Fresh Fields, and Wild Oats (for more stores: 800-449-4925 or www.ecover.com); Seventh Generation sold at Wild Oats, Whole People, and Shaw's (for more stores: 800-456-1191 or www.seventhgen.com); Sun and Earth sold at Pathmark (for more stores: 800-596-SAFE or www.sunandearth.com); Citrus Magic air freshener sold at Linens & Things, Kitchen Collection, and Petco, 888-583-6044 or www.petco.com (for more stores: 800-451-7096 or www.citrusmagic.com); Caldrea available at Gracious Home, 212-517-6300 (for more stores, 612-371-0003 or www.caldrea.com); page 134: Nature's Miracle sold at Petco, 888-583-6044 or www.petco.com (for more stores: 310-544-7125); Simple Green sold at Home Depot, Wal-Mart, and Kmart (for more stores: 800-228-0709 or www.simplegreen.com); for L'Occitane en Provence stores, 888-623-2880; Votivo Ltd. aromatic candles from Catoe & Bambu, NYC, 212-713-1502 (for more stores: 206-213-0966 or www.morningfarm.com); Diptyque candles available at Zitomer, NYC, 212-737-2016; for Aveda stores, 800-AVEDA24 or www.aveda.com; page 135: Earthbath Between Bath Deodorizing Spritz sold at Petco, 888-583-6044 or www.petco.com (for more stores: 415-771-1166 or www.earthbath.com); Vaska Herbal Fresh laundry powder available at Vaska Home, 510-548-2092 or www.vaskahome.com; Oh My Dog! fragrance available at Sephora, 877-SEPHORA, and Saks Fifth Avenue, NYC, 212-753-4000 or www.saksfifth-

avenue.com; rose water bottled by Cortas Canning & Refrigerating Co. available at Hannaford, 207-883-2911 or www.hannaford.com (for more stores: www.ziyad.com); Tomato Pick-Me-Up Cologne Spray and Tomato bath-and-body oil from Demeter Fragrance Library, NYC, 212-505-1535 or www.fashionplanet.com; page 136: terra-cotta lamp with candle from Caswell-Massey, 800-326-0500; Vornado and Bionaire products from Gracious Home, NYC, 212-517-6300 (for more stores: Vornado Air Circulation Systems Inc., 800-234-0604 or www.vornado.com; Bionaire Corp., 800-253-2764 or www.bionaireproducts.com); page 137: Pittsburgh Paints from Janovic Plaza, NYC, 800-772-4381 (for more stores: 888-774-1010); potted plant from Chelsea Garden Center, NYC, 212-929-2477; page 138: grass and bamboo arrangement from l'Olivier, NYC, 212-774-7676; page 140: Pet Music, 215-628-2300 or www.petmusic.com; Sentient Creatures, NYC, 212-865-5998; Rondout Valley Kennels, Accord, NY, 914-687-4406; page 139: Banana Republic peony fragrance, 888-906-2800 or www.bananarepublic.com; page 143: wood and fabric tree ornaments from the Terence Conran Shop, 212-755-9079; flowers by Michael George, NYC, 212-751-0689

10. PAWS FOR SAFETY

Page 147: Grannick's Bitter Apple spray and Bitter Apple cream taste deterrents from R.C. Steele, 800-872-3773 or www.rcsteele.com (for more stores: 203-854-4799 or www.grannicks.com); Indiglo night-light by Austin Innovations from Grey Supply, 800-867-2852 or www.topbulb.com; Window Filter by R.E.P. Industries, Lansdale, PA, from Service Hardware, NYC, 212-534-1510 (for more stores: 215-368-0154); page 148: Helmac Tacky Vac hand roller from Petco, 888-583-6044 or www.petco.com, and Lechter's, 800-326-1376 or www.lechters.com (for more stores: 800-435-6223 or www.evercare.com); page 149: Safe Paws ice melt available at Petco, 888-583-6044 or www.petco.com (for more stores, 800-783-7841); safety pool cover by Loop-Loc, Hauppauge, NY, 516-582-2626 or www.looploc.com; page 150: black polished river stones from Chelsea Garden Center, NYC, 212-929-2477; Kong from Petco, 888-583-6044 or www.petco.com (for more stores: 303-216-2626 or www.kongcompany.com); page 151: Wright On! catnip toy and cat scratcher/toy chest from George, San Francisco, CA, 415-441-0564 or Berkeley, CA, 510-644-1033 or www.georgesf.com (to request a George catalog: 877-344-5454); page 152: Planet Kong Xtreme Goodie Ball from Dogtoys.com (for more stores: 303-216-2626 or www.kongcompany.com); Abstract Bones by Blue Ribbon Dog Co. from the Terence Conran Shop, NYC, 212-755-9079 (for more stores: 212-736-9085); Nylabone Rhino from Drs. Foster & Smith, 800-826-7206 or www.drsfostersmith.com (for more stores: 732-988-8400 or www.tfh.com); Blitz Turbo Scratcher from Petco, 888-583-

6044 or www.petco.com; Karate Kat scratching post from the Pet Stop, NYC, 212-580-2400 (for more stores: 800-822-6628); JoRene Distributors, 888-6-JORENE or www.cattrees.com; Tiger Post from Angelical Cat Company, Sunrise, FL, 954-747-3629 or www.angelicalcat.com; rope-covered vase from Room, NYC, 888-420-ROOM or www.roomonline.com; page 153: Surreal Sticks by Blue Ribbon Dog Co. from the Terence Conran Shop, NYC, 212-755-9079; page 154: Worldwise corrugated-cardboard cat scratcher from Wal-Mart and Target stores (for more stores: 415-721-7400 or www.worldwise.com); page 155: Kitty Pod by Elizabeth Paige Smith from EPS Design, LA, 310-823-0291 or www.epsdesign.com; claw scratcher by Harry Allen, Harry Allen & Associates, NYC, 212-529-7239; page 157: white rubber vase by O from the Terence Conran Shop, NYC, 212-755-9079; Mother Earth painting by Nick Stavrides, 212-489-9418 or www.beinganartist.com; page 158: Draenert 1060 coffee table from Domus Design Collection, NYC, 212-685-0800 or www.ddcnyc.com; chrome laundry hamper with terry-cloth liner from Pottery Barn, 800-922-9934 or www.pottery-barn.com; Table Lamp from Blu Dot, Minneapolis, MN (for stores or catalog: 612-782-1844 or www.bludot.com); page 159: California Closets, 800-873-4264 or www.calclosets.com

Any ideas or suggestions on products or creative solutions to living stylishly with animals may be sent to Julia Szabo, c/o Bulfinch Press, 3 Center Plaza, Boston, MA 02108.

PICTURE CREDITS

John Gilliland
Pages 2, 4, 5, 9, 12, 13, 14, 16, 17, 18, 19, 22, 23, 25, 26, 28, 29, 31, 33, 35, 36, 38, 39, 40, 41, 43, 45, 46, 47, 49, 50, 51, 52 top, 53, 54, 55, 56, 57, 58, 60 bottom, 61, 62, 64 top, 65, 68, 69, 70 top, 72 bottom, 74, 75 right, 76, 77 bottom, 78, 81, 82, 83, 84 left, 86, 87, 90, 91, 92, 94, 96, 97, 99 top right, 100, 101, 102, 103, 105, 106 bottom, 107, 108 top, 111, 113, 115, 116 bottom, 117, 119 top, 120, 122, 126, 127, 128, 129, 131, 137, 138, 140, 141, 144, 145, 148, 149, 150 bottom, 151 top, 152, 153, 154, 156, 157 right, 159, 161, 162, 165, 166, 167, 168, 169, 172, 173

Pascal Blancon
Pages 21, 30, 42, 52 bottom, 59 top, 63, 64 bottom right, 73, 80 top, 84 right, 85, 93, 98, 108 bottom, 114, 116 top, 118, 121 left, 123, 124 top, 125, 132, 133, 134, 135 left and center, 142, 143, 147, 150 top, 157 left, 158 bottom, 171

Greg Broom
Pages 32, 34, 106 top, 112

Stan Wan
Pages 60 top, 71, 79, 80 bottom, 110, 119 bottom, 121 right, 124 bottom, 155 top and bottom right

Horace Long
Pages 64 bottom left, 104, 109, 170

Micheline Pelletier / Corbis Sygma
Page 24

Courtesy Mitchell Gold Company
Page 37

Antoine Bootz
Page 48

Dirk Westphal
Page 59 bottom, 67 top left

Copyright © 1998 by Sue Coe. Courtesy Galerie St. Etienne, New York.
Page 66 top left

Courtesy Debs & Co. Private collection, NYC
Page 66 top right

Courtesy James Graham & Sons, NYC / private collection
Page 66 bottom

Courtesy of Mr. and Mrs. Greg Selch, NY
Page 67 bottom

Courtesy Bowman Hastie
Page 67 top right

Peter Aaron / Esto Photographics Inc.
Page 70 bottom

Drawing courtesy Sara Lopergolo, G and L Architects, NY
Page 71

Jeff Goldberg / Esto Photographics Inc.
Page 72 top

Dan Forer / Forer Inc.
Page 75 left

Joachim Magrean
Page 77 top, 89

Ivan Terestchenko
Page 95

Courtesy Möbelform
Page 99 top left

The Metropolitan Museum of Art, gift of Mr. and Mrs. Charles Wrightsman, 1971
Page 99 bottom

Mark Platt
Page 135 right

Courtesy Banana Republic
Page 139

Courtesy George
Page 151 bottom

Lynn Campbell
Page 155 bottom left

© Fotostudio Faaber
Page 158 top